Tadpole Tales
and Other Totally Terrific Treats
for Readers Theatre

Tadpole Tales
and Other Totally Terrific Treats
for Readers Theatre

Anthony D. Fredericks

Illustrated by
Anthony Allan Stoner

1997
TEACHER IDEAS PRESS
A Member of Greenwood Publishing, Inc.
Westport, Connecticut • London

To Pete Piepmeier
for his warm friendship,
sincere support,
and infectious good humor . . .
may they always be celebrated!

TEACHER IDEAS PRESS
A member of Greenwood Publishing Group, Inc.
88 Post Road West,
Westport, CT 06881
www.lu.com

Production Editor: Stephen Haenel
Copy Editor: Jan Krygier
Proofreader: Suzanne Hawkins Burke
Interior Design and Layout: Judy Gay Matthews

Library of Congress Cataloging-in-Publication Data

Fredericks, Anthony D.
   Tadpole tales and other totally terrific treats for readers
theatre / Anthony D. Fredericks.
      xiv, 140 p.   22x28 cm.
      Includes bibliographical references (p. 123)
      ISBN 1-56308-547-X
      1. Readers' theater.   2. Mother Goose--Parodies, imitations, etc.
   3. Fairy tales--Parodies, imitations, etc.   I. Title.
PN2081.R4F75   1997
372.67'6--dc21   97-31102
                                                                        CIP

10 9 8 7 6 5 4

Contents

Part I
THE BEGINNING OF THE BOOK
(Well, almost)

Part II
THIS IS THE MAIN PART OF THE BOOK—
THE SECTION WITH ALL
THE WONDERFULLY CREATIVE
(AND VERY STRANGE)
STORIES YOU BOUGHT THIS BOOK FOR

Part III
SWIM ON OVER . . .
HERE'S A BUNCH OF TADPOLE TALES
(or should that be "Tadpole Tails?")

Part IV
THIS IS THE SECTION OF THE BOOK
THAT HAS SOME UNFINISHED SCRIPTS
AND PARTIAL STORIES
FOR YOUR STUDENTS TO COMPLETE
(Pretty neat idea, huh?)

**Part V
APPENDIXES
(The stuff you always find
at the end of a book)**

Here's the PREFACE Part of the Book Where You Can Find out How This Book Came to Be Written and Other Stuff About Me and My Tadpole Friends

Once upon a time, way back in 1993, I wrote a book called *Frantic Frogs and Other Frankly Fractured Folktales for Readers Theatre* (and you thought the title of *this* book was weird!). That book was (and still is) a collection of really bizarre, peculiar, odd, wacky, and far-out retellings of popular and well-known children's stories presented in a readers theatre format. Titles of some of the scripts in that book include:

- Beauty and This Incredibly Ugly Guy

- Don't Kiss Sleeping Beauty, She's Got Really Bad Breath

- Coughy, the Dwarf Snow White Never Told You About

- Jack Climbs to the Top of a Very Tall Vegetable and Finds a Very Large Individual with an Attitude Problem

- Rumplestiltskin Tries to Spell His Name

- Rapunzel Gets a Really Lousy Hairdo

(As you can probably tell by now, I've got this completely and totally warped sense of humor—but let's not get into *all* of my personality defects just yet.)

Anyway, as I was saying, I wrote that book, and it soon found its way into catalogs, bookstores, and educational conferences around the country. It wasn't long before it was, as they like to say in the publishing business, "selling like hotcakes." Teachers would buy it and use it as a major part of their language arts program. Librarians would buy it and use it to introduce familiar fairy tales and legends as part of a summer reading program. Even parents would buy it to share with their children during family read-alouds.

One of the magical benefits of writing that book was that I was invited into classrooms to watch various groups of students present readers theatre performances. (If that isn't a "high" for an author, then I don't know what is!) It was always gratifying to watch the overwhelming jubilation and uncontrollable laughter that accompanied those presentations . . . not to mention the uncontrollable classes that resulted when any of them put on a "frankly fractured folktale" for a group of visitors. (I'm sure my name is "Mud" to many elementary school principals across the country.)

Letters I received from teachers, librarians, and kids attested to the unbelievable joy and unmatched hilarity that permeated classrooms from coast to coast. One teacher wrote, "I've never had so much fun teaching language arts as I did with this book." Another wrote, "What an incredible book! My students couldn't stop laughing for days." A class of fourth graders wrote a two-word letter which simply said: "More, please!" Wow! Was I excited!

(Interestingly, one of the great benefits of that book was the way in which it stimulated and supported kids' writing efforts. Included in that book (as in this one) are partial scripts for kids to finish on their own as well as a collection of silly and foolish titles for kids to use in developing their own stories from scratch. Students all over the country were participating in the writing process in very creative and dynamic ways.)

With the success of *Frantic Frogs* . . . it wasn't too long before teachers and colleagues began approaching me at educational conferences and conventions to ask for a new volume of wild and wacky readers theatre scripts (of course, there were others who said that they never wanted to see my face in their town again—but, that's another story). As *Frantic Frogs* . . . was written for students in grades 4–8, many primary-level teachers wanted their own book of absurd, ridiculous, and totally insane readers theatre scripts that they could use in their classrooms.

Thus was born the idea for this book—a collection of crazy, irreverent, demented, outrageous, gross scripts that kids in grades 1–4 can use as part of their language arts program. As if that weren't clever enough, the scripts are actually divided by reading level. (Check the Contents.) I figured that many kids had heard of Mother Goose, but how many have heard of the story "Old Mother Hubbard went to the Cupboard and Got Sick at What She Saw?" Most kids are probably familiar with the version of Humpty Dumpty falling off the wall but not the version about him becoming a short-order cook at McDonald's. And lots of youngsters know the traditional version of "Mary Had a Little Lamb" but may not be familiar with the more gritty tale "Mary Had a Little Lamb That Made a Big 'No-No' on the Classroom Floor."

Actually, the title for this book was not my idea. It rightfully belongs to a most wonderful, delightful, magnificent, dynamic, marvelous editorial-type person at Teacher Ideas Press—Jo Anne Ricca. Her multitalented and incredibly creative gray matter (i.e., brain) thought that because *Frantic Frogs* . . . had been written for intermediate-level students, the sequel (or prequel, depending on your perspective) for primary-level students should appropriately have the word *Tadpoles* in its title. (It's simply amazing how the warped sense of humor of my editors is so in sync with mine!) As an astute reader, you'll also note that this literary series is beginning to look like a form of reverse metamorphosis (Frog→Tadpole→etc.)—a fact that I'm sure is causing Mr. Darwin to be turning in his grave. I suspect that the next book in this series will carry a title such as *Eager Eggs and Other Enthusiastically Earnest Entries for Readers Theatre* and will be written for newborns and infants. The book after that . . . well, please don't ask!

This is all a roundabout way of telling you how much fun I had in writing the first book (and how much fun others have had in using it) and how that convoluted view of traditional children's stories and other fairy tale characters has been continued in the pages of this volume. I sincerely hope that you find the scripts in this book to be as welcome and amusing as those in *Frantic Frogs* . . . and that they will energize your students with an overwhelming abundance of hilarity, humor, amusement, fun, jocularity, and infectious good times.

Here's to lots of laughter, lots of learning, and lots of just plain craziness!!! May your classroom or library be filled with all three.

—Tony Fredericks

Acknowledgments
(or, Thanks for the Memories)

WOW! So many folks and so little time . . . .

To all the readers of *Frantic Frogs and Other Frankly Fractured Folktales for Readers Theatre*—I humbly stand before you on bended knee (now there's a neat trick!) with appreciation for all your wonderful responses about the laughter and hilarity that filled your classrooms with that book.

A note of sympathy to Mrs. Dumpty who had to put up with throngs of newspaper reporters and TV broadcasters after that unfortunate incident at the wall. (I still think one of the king's horses did it.)

To Peter Peterpumpkineater who finally moved the family to a condo in the suburbs after their original one got just a little too . . . well, you know what I mean.

To Jack and Jill and their endless trips to that ever-present well at the top of the hill. (Hey, have you guys ever thought about indoor plumbing?)

To Susan Zernial for her continued support, encouragement, and delightful propensity for keeping me permanently parked in front of my word processor.

To Little Miss Muffet who throws one mean party with all that curds and whey and stuff. (By the way, did you ever find out what happened to the spider and her date, the fly?)

To Sleeping Beauty who *R-E-A-L-L-Y* needs to invest in some serious mouthwash if she ever thinks she's going to land one of those handsome prince guys down at the castle.

To Old Mother Hubbard who spends her entire day opening up empty cupboard doors . . . and her poor little poopsie woopsie who never gets anything to eat for dinner.

To Mr. and Mrs. Old MacDonald who allowed me to interview all the guys in the barnyard for the *National Inquisitor* article about how alien beings were teaching farm animals to talk.

To kids everywhere whose silliness is the inspiration for these stories, whose craziness is the eternal stimulus for one middle-aged writer, whose wackiness fills classrooms with perpetual frivolity, and whose enthusiasm makes teaching such a constant joy.

Part I

THE BEGINNING OF THE BOOK
(Well, almost)

This Is the INTRODUCTION Part of the Book Which Tells You Some Really IMPORTANT STUFF About HOW TO USE THIS BOOK (and All the Really Neat Stories) in Your CLASSROOM or LIBRARY

"Once upon a time . . ."

Certainly these must be the four most wondrous words in the English language (or any language, for that matter). These words conjure up all sorts of visions and possibilities—faraway lands, magnificent adventures, enchanted princes, beautiful princesses, evil wizards and wicked witches, a few dragons and demons, a couple of castles and cottages, perhaps a mysterious forest or two, and certainly tales of mystery, intrigue, and adventure. These are stories of tradition and timelessness, tales that enchant, mystify, and excite through a marvelous weaving of characters, settings, and plots—tales that have stood the test of time. These are stories of our youth, stories of our heritage, and stories that continue to enrapture audiences with their delightful blending of good over evil, patience over greed, and right over might. Our senses are stimulated, our mental images are energized, and our experiences are fortified with that most magical preface—"Once upon a time . . . ."

The magic of storytelling has been a tradition of every culture and civilization since the dawn of language. It binds human beings and celebrates their heritage as no other language art can. It is part and parcel of the human experience, because it underscores the values and experiences we cherish as well as those we seek to share with each other. Nowhere is this more necessary than in today's classroom. Young children, who have been bombarded with visual messages (i.e., television) since birth, still relish and appreciate the power and majesty of a story well told. Even adults, immersed in their hustle-and-bustle lifestyles, enjoy the magic of a story or the enchantment of a storyteller. Perhaps it is a natural part of who we are that stories command our attention and help us appreciate the values, ideas, and traditions we hold dear. So, too, should children have those same experiences and those same pleasures.

What Is Readers Theatre?

Readers theatre is a storytelling device that stimulates the imagination and promotes *all* of the language arts. Simply stated, it is an oral interpretation of a piece of literature read in a dramatic style. But its value extends far beyond that simple definition. It is an act of involvement, an opportunity to share, a time to creatively interact with others, and a personal interpretation of what can be or could be. Here's another definition of readers theatre:

Readers Theatre is an interpretive reading activity for all the children in the classroom. Readers bring characters to life through their voices and gestures. Listeners are captivated by the vitalized stories and complete the activity by imagining the details of scene and action. . . . Used in the classroom, Readers Theatre becomes an integrated language event centering upon oral interpretation of literature. The children adapt and present the material of their choice. A story, a poem, a scene from a play, even a song lyric, provides the ingredients for the script. As a thinking, reading, writing, speaking and listening experience, Readers Theatre makes a unique contribution to our language arts curriculum. (Sloyer, 1982, p. 3)

It is evident that readers theatre holds the promise of helping children understand and appreciate the richness of language, the ways in which to interpret that language, and how language can be a powerful vehicle for the comprehension and appreciation of different forms of literature. Readers theatre provides numerous opportunities for youngsters to make stories and literature come alive and pulsate with their own unique brand of interpretation and vision. In so doing, literature provides children with a plethora of opportunities to be authentic users of language.

What Is the Value of Readers Theatre?

I like to think of readers theatre as a way to interpret literature without the constraints of skill levels, memorization, or artificial structures (e.g., lots of props, costumes, elaborate staging). Readers theatre allows children to breathe life and substance into literature—to give it an interpretation that is neither right nor wrong, as it will be colored by their unique perspectives, experiences, and vision. It is, in fact, the readers' interpretation of a piece of literature or a familiar story that is intrinsically more valuable than some predetermined or preordained translation (something that might be found in a teacher's manual or curriculum guide, for example).

With that in mind, I'd like to share with you some of the many values I see in readers theatre:

- It stimulates curiosity and enthusiasm for different forms of literature. It allows children to experiences stories in a supportive and nonthreatening format that underscores their active involvement.

- Because readers theatre allows children many different interpretations of the same story, it facilitates the development of critical and creative thinking. Because there is no such thing as a "right" or "wrong" interpretation of a story, children can stretch their thinking beyond the boundries imposed on them by traditional language arts curricula.

- Readers theatre focuses on all of the language arts—reading, writing, speaking, and listening. It supports a holistic philosophy of instruction and allows children to become responsible learners who seek out answers to their own self-initiated inquiries.

- Because it is the performance that drives readers theatre, children are given more opportunities to invest themselves and their personalities in the production of a readers theatre. The same story may be subject to several different presentations depending on the group or the individual youngsters involved. As such, children learn that readers theatre (like other forms of literature) can be explored in a host of ways and a host of possibilities.

- Children are given numerous opportunities to learn about the major features of children's literature—plot, theme, setting, point of view, and characterization. This is particularly so when they are provided with opportunities to design and construct their own readers theatre scripts and have unlimited opportunities to discover the wide variations that can be used with a single piece.

- Readers theatre is a participatory event. The characters as well as the audience are all intimately involved in the design, structure, and delivery of the story. As such, children begin to realize that reading is not a solitary activity but one that can be shared and discussed with others.

- Readers theatre is informal and relaxed. It does not require elaborate props, scenery, or costumes. It can be set up in any classroom or library. It does not require large sums of money to "make it happen." And, it can take place in any kind of environment—formal or informal.

- Readers theatre stimulates the imagination and the creation of visual images. It has been substantiated that when youngsters are provided with opportunities to create their own mental images, their comprehension and appreciation of a piece of writing increase dramatically. Because only a modicum of formal props and setup is required for any readers theatre production, the participants and audience are encouraged to create supplemental props in their minds—props that may be more elaborate and exquisite than those found in the most lavish plays.

- Readers theatre enhances the development of cooperative learning strategies. It requires youngsters to work together toward a common goal and supports their efforts in doing so. Readers theatre is not a competitive activity but rather a cooperative one in which children share, discuss, and band together for the good of the production.

- Readers theatre is valuable for non-English-speaking children or nonfluent readers. It provides them with positive models of language usage and interpretation that extend far beyond the decoding of printed materials. It allows them to see language in action and the various ways in which language can be used.

- Teachers and librarians have discovered that readers theatre is an excellent way in which to enhance the development of communication skills. Voice projection, intonation, inflection, and pronunciation skills are all promoted within and throughout any readers theatre production. Children who need assistance in these areas are provided with a support structure that encourages the development of necessary abilities.

- The development and enhancement of self-concept is facilitated through readers theatre. Because children are working in concert with other children in a supportive atmosphere, their self-esteem mushrooms accordingly. Again, the emphasis is on the presentation, not the performers. As such, youngsters have opportunities to develop levels of self-confidence and self-assurance that would not normally be available in more traditional class productions.

- Creative and critical thinking are enhanced through the use of readers theatre. Children are active participants in the interpretation and delivery of a story; as such, they develop thinking skills that are divergent rather than convergent, and interpretive skills that are supported rather than directed.

- When children are provided with opportunities to write or script their own readers theatre, their writing abilities are supported and encouraged. As children become familiar with the design and format of readers theatre scripts, they can begin to use their own creative talents in designing scripts and stories.

- Readers theatre is fun. Children of all ages have delighted in using readers theatre for many years. It is enjoyable and stimulating, encouraging and fascinating, relevant and personal. Indeed, try as I might, I have not been able to locate a single instance (or group of children) in which (or for whom) readers theatre would not be an appropriate language arts activity. It offers a cornucopia of possibilities and promises.

How to Present Readers Theatre

It is important to remember that there is no single way to present readers theatre. What I will share with you here are some considerations you and the youngsters with whom you work may wish to keep in mind as you put on one of the productions in this book. Different classes, and even different groups of children within the same class, will have their own method and mode of presentation; in other words, no two presentations may ever be the same. However, there are some elements common to all readers theatre presentations:

- Much of the setting for a story should take place in the audience's mind. Elaborate scenes or scenery are not necessary. A branch or potted plant can serve as a tree; a paper cutout can serve as a tie, badge, or some other attachment; and a hand-lettered sign can be used to designate one part of the staging area as a particular scene (e.g., a swamp, a castle, a field, a forest).

- Usually all of the characters will remain on stage throughout the presentation. If you place the characters on stools, they can face the audience when they are involved in a particular scene and then turn around whenever they are not involved in a scene. You may wish to make simple hand-lettered signs with the names of each character. Loop a piece of string or yarn through each sign and hang it around the neck of the respective character. The audience then will know the identity of each character throughout the presentation.

- Several presentations use a narrator to set up the story. The narrator establishes the place and time of the story for the audience so that the characters can "jump into" their parts from the beginning of the story. Typically, the narrator is separated from the other actors and can be identified by a simple sign.

- A copy of the script should be provided for each actor. Each script can be bound between two sheets of colored construction paper or poster board. Bound scripts tend to formalize the presentation a little and lend an air of professionalism to the actors. You may wish to highlight each character's speaking parts with different color highlighter pens.

- The readers should have an opportunity to practice their script before presenting it to an audience. Take some time to discuss voice intonation, facial gestures, body movements, and other features that could be used to enhance the presentation. Be encouraging in allowing the children the opportunity to suggest their own modifications, adaptations, or interpretations of the script. They will undoubtedly be in touch with the interests and perceptions of their peers and can offer some distinctive and personal interpretations.

- The characters should focus on the audience rather than on each other. Practicing the script beforehand can eliminate this problem and help the children understand the need to involve the audience as much as possible in the development of the story. Here, voice projection and delivery are important in allowing the audience to understand each character's actions. The proper mood and intent need to be established, and this can be done only when the children are familiar and comfortable with each character's "style."

- Children should *not* memorize their lines but should rehearse them sufficiently so that they are comfortable with them. Again, the emphasis is on delivery, so be sure to suggest different types of voice (e.g., angry, irritated, calm, frustrated, excited) for the children to use for their particular character(s).

Presenting a readers theatre script need not be an elaborate or extensive production. As children become more familiar and polished in using readers theatre, they will be able to suggest a multitude of presentation possibilities for future scripts. It is important to help children assume a measure of responsibility for the delivery of any readers theatre. In so doing, you will be helping to ensure their personal engagement and active participation in this most valuable of language arts activities.

How to Create Your Own Readers Theatre

It is hoped that you and your students will find an abundance of readers theatre scripts in this book for use in your own classroom. But these scripts should also serve as an impetus for the creation of your own classroom or library scripts. By providing opportunities for your children to begin designing their own readers theatre scripts, you will be offering them an exciting new arena in which to demonstrate and enhance their writing abilities.

Following are some suggestions you and your students may wish to consider in developing your own readers theatre scripts. They are purposely generic in nature and can be used with almost all kinds of reading material. Of course, the emphasis in this book is on humorous readers theatre scripts, particularly those dealing with fairy tales, Mother Goose rhymes, fables, legends, and other children's classics; thus, these ideas will help children create their own fractured fairy tales as part of their process writing program.

Select an Appropriate Story

Humor works best when it touches something with which we are familiar. For this reason, the stories selected for this book have come from the experiential background of most children—Mother Goose, legends, tall tales, fairy tales, and the like—and have then been expanded far beyond their original design. The stories children select for the development of their own readers theatre scripts should also be familiar ones. In so doing, they will be able to build on that familiarity for a humorous effect.

Appendix A is a bibliography of fairy tales, books, and stories that will provide you with some possibilities and ideas for use in the creation of original readers theatre scripts. These examples represent a wide range of stories from many different lands and many different times. An attempt has been made to include familiar tales as well as others that children will enjoy. All of the listed stories and tales have been selected for their dramatic appeal and their adaptability to a readers theatre script. I have found, however, that most, if not all, fairy tales and Mother Goose rhymes can be adapted to a readers theatre format . . . depending on how warped one's sense of humor is. Nevertheless, the **best kind** of stories to use are those with tight plots and clear endings, distinctive characters, engaging dialogue, and universal themes (e.g., good prevails over evil, love conquers all, logic is more powerful than physical strength).

In selecting stories, the number of characters needs to be considered as well. I have found that two to six characters works best. For that reason, some minor characters may be eliminated and their dialogue absorbed by other characters; on the other hand, one or two brand new characters may need to be developed to facilitate the pace of the story. It is important that the staging area is not crowded with too many characters, thus hindering the audience's attention.

Illustrate and Model

Initially, children may be unfamiliar with the format of readers theatre. It is important to discuss with children the fact that readers theatre scripts are very similar to movie and television scripts and are written in much the same way. As in Hollywood, the intent is to take a basic story and turn it into a play or movie. With your children, discuss the original stories used as the foundation of these scripts and the resultant readers theatre design(s).

Lead the class in a whole group activity to model the steps used in designing a readers theatre script. I have found it advantageous to use a sheet of chart pack paper, a large piece of poster board, or the overhead projector. Using a familiar story, I begin to rewrite it so that the entire group can see the steps I use. These steps might include:

rewriting the title to give it a more humorous slant;

eliminating unnecessary dialogue or minor characters;

inserting a narrator at strategic points to advance the action or identify specific scenes;

adding words that describe the tone of voice used by a specific character (e.g., *rapidly, irritated, confused*);

underlining or bold-facing the names of characters for easy identification;

creating new dialogue, characters, or settings to advance the story or produce a humorous situation; and

noting props necessary for the story.

It should be pointed out that there is no ideal series of steps to follow in the design of readers theatre scripts. It is important, however, that children have some models to follow so that they will be encouraged and supported in the creation of their own scripts.

Adapting the Story

After the children have experienced the scripts in this book they will be familiar with ways in which a familiar fairy tale or legend can be turned into a humorous readers theatre script. When you allow children opportunities to develop their own humorous scripts, you will soon discover a wonderfully creative spirit permeating all aspects of your language arts program.

Obviously, humor comes in many forms. Here are some methods you and your students may wish to consider in transforming familiar tales into wild and wacky ones:

Exaggeration. Blow something completely out of proportion. Instead of "Little Boy Blue," title a revised version "Just Another Tale About Some Kid Who Dresses Up in Blue and Sleeps in Haystacks." In place of "Humpty Dumpty," use "This Very Round Fellow Who Sits on Top of a Wall All Day Long." Exaggeration can extend beyond story titles to character personalities and physical descriptions, as well as story settings.

Colloquialisms. Allow the children to use language and idioms with which they are most familiar (subject to teacher approval). Slang terms and phrases in the mouths of familiar characters can be quite funny. For example, Simple Simon could say, "Hey, dude, would you like to have some 'Ding Dongs' instead of pie?" Or, one of the Three Blind Mice could say, "Hey, stop buggin' us. We've had it up to here with that woman chasing us with a knife." Obviously, a selective use of colloquialisms is preferable to a script rife with slang.

Reversals. Change characters' personalities so that they are completely different. For example, instead of the typical evil stepmother, have the children create a really nice stepmother; instead of an enchanted prince, have the children develop a stupid prince; instead of a fire-breathing dragon, have the children create a shy reptile trying to kick the smoking habit. Reversals (or partial reversals) can be used for the settings of stories, too. Instead of a gingerbread house, have the children design a condo in the suburbs; instead of a farmhouse, have the children use a beach hut in Hawaii; instead of a deep, dark forest, have the children set a story in a shopping mall.

Anachronisms. Use an object that is totally out of place in the story. For example, instead of having the wicked witch travel on a broomstick, allow her to use her frequent flyer miles to travel by airplane; instead of having characters travel from one castle to another, have them call each other using their cellular phones; instead of the main character sending a poison pen letter by messenger, have it faxed.

Misdirection. Misdirection occurs when the reader or listener is misled as to the outcome of a story. For example, the story of Old Mother Hubbard could end with the dog looking for food for the old woman, or Little Miss Muffet could eat fried spiders instead of curds and whey.

Character changes. Give familiar characters entirely new personalities or whole new physical features. For example, Humpty Dumpty could give up his day job to work as a short-order cook at McDonald's. The fire-breathing dragon could get a loan from the bank and market his own brand of barbecue sauce. The old woman in the shoe could branch out and build a condo complex of sneakers and pumps. The troll could go to charm school and learn to eat with a knife and fork.

Combination formula. Using a combination formula, the writer combines two very different subjects or elements into an entirely new arrangement. For example, the eating habits of a frog can be combined with the eating habits of a prince to create a prince who sits around the castle all day snatching flies out of the air with his three-foot tongue. The personality of a mouse can be combined with the personality of a real estate developer to create a small rodent who sells nests to families of rats. The features of a fairy tale cottage can be combined with the features of a suburban housing development to create a development of condos for wicked witches only (no young children allowed).

Preparation and Writing

Children should be encouraged to work together to design their readers theatre scripts. Small groups of four or five children will allow for a multiplicity of options and suggestions for scripting a familiar story. It would be advantageous to appoint one youngster within each group to serve as the "scribe," "reporter," or "recorder." Each recorder should understand that writing goes through many stages and that the first couple of ideas are just that—initial ideas can be eliminated or expanded according to the wishes and desires of the group.

Have each group's recorder write the names of all the identified characters down the left side of a large sheet of poster paper. Other members of the group can suggest possible dialogue for each of the characters as well as the narrator. Movements and actions can also be suggested by group members. I have found it advantageous to hold off considering any props, stage directions, and setup until after the initial draft of the script is complete. In this way, children can concentrate on the creative expression of their ideas without worrying about some of the minor aspects of their script, all of which can be added later.

Production and Practice

Provide student groups with opportunities to try out their drafts on other groups of children. They should pay special attention to the flow of the story, the pace, appropriate dialogue, and, of course, the humor of their script. Just as a playwright will go through many drafts of a play, so too should children realize that they may also need time to work out the kinks in their productions. By trying out their various drafts on other children, they will have an opportunity to structure and restructure their readers theatre script for maximum impact.

Yes, We Even Have a Section on Evaluation!

To be effective, evaluation must be a continuous process. It must also engage children in the design of their own learning objectives and provide teachers, librarians, and children with useful data that can be used to enhance learning opportunities. In that light, evaluation is much more than the traditional pen-and-paper tests of yesterday; rather, it is a process of reaction, reflection, and redirection that should have a positive impact on children's literacy growth and development.

Any effective evaluation program will have the following characteristics:

- It will be continuous and ongoing; it will be a constant process of evolution.

- It will emphasize a variety of evaluative tools and devices in line with children's different needs, abilities, and interests.

- It will promote a collaborative spirit between and among children and teachers. It will not be something *done to* children but something *done with* children.

- It will be authentic in nature, reflective of children's developing literacy skills, and supportive of their self-initiated ventures into the world of books and literature.

I'm certainly not suggesting that you need to initiate a new form of evaluation solely for readers theatre activities. Nor do I mean to imply that readers theatre even needs to be evaluated with some of the more traditional methods. Readers theatre, in and of itself, should be a pleasurable and stimulating experience for children. Attaching an evaluation component to each and every readers theatre script may rob children of the excitement and spontaneity that so often permeate this language arts activity.

However, if you are interested in using readers theatre as a regular part of a language arts program, you may wish to consider some of the following as appropriate criteria in your evaluation process. This list is certainly not meant to be finite or complete. It's important that you also talk with students about other evaluative measures that support the four guidelines suggested above.

- After a presentation, have all members of the class discuss the impact of the story. What could be done to improve it? Why? Any suggested changes or modifications?

- Use anecdotal records to record the participation of members of the cast as well as members of the audience. Teachers may wish to answer the following: Were students engaged? Were students excited? Were students actively involved?

- Provide several members of the audience with feedback forms in which they respond to such elements as (1) expression, (2) involvement, (3) presentation, and (4) level of excitement generated by the performance.

- Identify three or four children in the audience to mark a "yes or no" checklist which has been designed by the whole class. The checklist can be turned over to cast members who can then use it as a part of their own evaluation of the performance.

- Have individuals from other classes complete simple observational records designed by you.

- Shoot photographs or a video of a specific presentation for later analysis by cast members or the whole class.

- Have each "production team" develop self-assessment forms. These can be discussed by the cast after a presentation and their findings shared with the entire class.

- Have a group of children maintain a project log, including the drafting, preparation, and presentation of a readers theatre script. The log can become part of a larger classroom portfolio or turned over to the teacher for comments and discussion.

- The student members of a production crew can each maintain a reading response log in which they record their thoughts and perceptions about the development and presentation of a specific readers theatre script.

Evaluation should offer children opportunities for growth and improvement. As stated above, however, it is certainly not necessary or essential to evaluate everything your children do related to readers theatre. It is important that you are sensitive to the interest factor involved with readers theatre and not diminish it by constant assessment and evaluation. Be aware that evaluation affects children's developing self-concepts as much as their developing academic skills. *How* you evaluate is just as important as *what* you evaluate.

References

Fredericks, Anthony D. *Frantic Frogs and Other Frankly Fractured Folktales for Readers Theatre.* Englewood, Colo.: Teacher Ideas Press, 1993.

Sloyer, Shirley. *Readers Theatre: Story Dramatization in the Classroom.* Urbana, Ill.: National Council of Teachers of English, 1982.

Part II

THIS IS THE MAIN PART OF THE BOOK—
THE SECTION WITH ALL
THE WONDERFULLY CREATIVE
(AND VERY STRANGE)
STORIES YOU BOUGHT THIS BOOK FOR

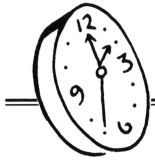

Hickory Dickory Dock, the Mouse Ran up the Clock— But He Couldn't Tell Time

STAGING: The narrator can stand or sit off to the side. The characters can be seated on stools or standing.

Narrator
X

                                                Mouse   *Clock*
                                                  X   *X*

NARRATOR: Once upon a time there was this mouse. For some reason he needed to know what time it was. I guess he had a doctor's appointment, or he had to get a book back to the library. Anyway, he was running around the house. Suddenly, he saw a tall clock in the corner.

MOUSE: I think I'll climb up that tall clock and find out what time it is.

NARRATOR: So the mouse began to run up the clock.

CLOCK: Hey, stop that. That tickles!

MOUSE: All I want to do is find out what time it is.

CLOCK: Why don't you get a watch or something?

MOUSE: How am I going to wear a watch? My wrist is much too small.

CLOCK: What about a pocket watch?

MOUSE:	Are you kidding? If you look real hard, you'll notice that I'm not wearing any pants. Where would I put a pocket watch?
CLOCK:	How about an alarm clock by your bed?
MOUSE:	You must be joking! I sleep on a dirty old floor in a hole in the wall. I don't even have a bed. What good is an alarm clock going to do me?
CLOCK:	What about the clock on the microwave oven in your kitchen?
MOUSE:	Now I know you're kidding. What would a mouse do with a microwave oven? All we get to eat is dirty old cheese and leftover scraps of food. And, besides, we could never afford the price of a microwave oven.
CLOCK:	Well, I'm sorry, pal. I just can't help you anymore. You're going to have to find out what time it is some other way. When you run up and down me, I just want to giggle and laugh and snicker . . . especially when you prance across the front of me.
NARRATOR:	The mouse then gets a brilliant idea. He starts to run back and forth across the front of the clock.
CLOCK:	Ha, ha, ha, hee, hee, hee, ho, ho, ho.
NARRATOR:	The mouse continues tickling the clock.
CLOCK:	Ha, ha, ha, ha, ha, hee, hee, hee, hee, hee, ho, ho, ho, ho, ho. Stop it! Stop it! Stop it! Stop it!
NARRATOR:	The mouse tickles the clock some more.

CLOCK: Ha, ha, ha, ha, ha, hee, hee, hee, hee, hee, ho, ho, ho, ho, ho. Stop it! Stop it! Stop it! I can't stand it anymore. OK, OK, I give up.

MOUSE: Will you let me run up your face and find out what time it is?

CLOCK: Yes, go ahead. But make it quick.

NARRATOR: And so the mouse ran up the front of the clock. But when he got to the top, he remembered that he never learned how to tell time. So he had to run back down again. A few weeks later, in school, he finally learned how to tell time. Then he and the clock became best friends. In fact, they had the greatest time together.

CLOCK: Ha, ha, ha, hee, hee, hee, ho, ho, ho.

The Three Blind Mice Get Smart (Almost)

STAGING: The narrator can stand off to one side of the staging area. The characters should be standing and may wish to walk around as they are saying their lines. If possible, have the three mice wear sunglasses.

Mouse #1
X

Farmer's Wife
X

Mouse #2
X

Mouse #3
X

Narrator
X

NARRATOR:	Three blind mice, three blind mice See how they run, see how they run! They all ran after the farmer's wife, Who cut off their tails with a carving knife. Did you ever see such a sight in your life As three blind mice?
MOUSE #1:	Hey look, guys. We're really taking it in the chops. First of all, we can't see. Then we have this crazy woman chasing after us with a knife. Then she goes and cuts off our tails.
MOUSE #2:	You're right. We are really getting beat up by that crazy lady.
MOUSE #3:	You said it! What do you think is going to happen next?
MOUSE #2:	Maybe we'll get run over by a runaway tractor.

22

MOUSE #1:	Or maybe the cat will hang us up in a tree to be pecked at by birds.
MOUSE #3:	Or maybe the farmer's kid will put us in the blender and make mouse shakes.
MOUSE #2:	It's sure getting dangerous around here.
MOUSE #3:	You're not kidding!
MOUSE #1:	So, what do we do? If we show our faces, that crazy lady will come after us again.
FARMER'S WIFE:	Now just wait a gosh darn minute. I'm not crazy. I'm only doing my job. You heard what the narrator said. I have to chase after you guys with a sharp object. So don't blame me for all your troubles. Blame the writer.
MOUSE #2:	Listen, lady, just stay away from us.
NARRATOR:	The three mice get together to talk about the problem. After several minutes, they form a plan.
MOUSE #1:	OK, guys, here it is. Let's tie a giant bell around her neck. Then, we'll be able to hear her coming. And we'll have time to escape.
MOUSE #3:	That's a great plan, except for one little thing.
MOUSE #1:	What's that?
MOUSE #3:	Because we can't see, how are we going to tie the bell around her neck?
MOUSE #1:	Gosh, we never thought about that.

MOUSE #2: Well, guys, I guess we go back to having the crazy lady chase us all over the house.

MOUSE #1: So much for that idea!

NARRATOR: Three blind mice, three blind mice
See how they run, see how they run!
They all ran after the farmer's wife,
Who cut off their tails with a carving knife.
Did you ever see such a sight in your life
As three blind mice?

One, Two, Buckle My Shoe.
Three, Four,
Mommy Can Snore

STAGING: The characters can be seated on chairs or stools. The narrator should be off to the side and can be at a podium. Throughout the entire telling of the story, loud snores should be coming from off stage.

<table>
<tr><td></td><td>Kid #1
X</td><td>Kid #2
X</td><td>Kid #3
X</td></tr>
</table>

Narrator
X

NARRATOR:	One, two, buckle my shoe. Three, four, shut the . . . .
KID #1:	*(interrupting)* Whoa there, oh great Narrator. Before you break into song, I think I'd better tell you something.
NARRATOR:	What's that?
KID #1:	Well, if you listen very carefully, you might hear something very strange, very loud, and very irritating.
KID #2:	Yeah, and you know what else. It's been going on for quite a long time.
KID #3:	All Mother does is snore, snore, snore. We can't get her to stop.
NARRATOR:	Now look, that's not my problem. I was hired to tell everybody out there *(points to the audience)* a couple of Mother Goose rhymes and entertain them for a while.

KID #1:   Yeah, we know. But, you see, there's something you probably don't know.

NARRATOR: What's that?

KID #2:   Well, you see . . . it's, ah . . . well . . . I mean . . . it's . . . ah . . . .

KID #3:   What my not-too-bright friend here is trying to tell you is that the mother that is doing all that snoring is not really our mother.

KID #1:   Yeah, you see it's really the mother of all mothers—you know—Mother Goose.

NARRATOR: You mean . . . .

KID #3:   That's right, oh great and wonderful narrator person. It's none other than the old lady herself, snoring away like one giant foghorn.

KID #1: I guess she thought that once she finished writing all those rhymes, and once all those rhymes got published in a book, and once that book was bought by all those children, and once all those children read that book, and once . . . .

KID #2: Hey, will you please just get to the point!

KID #1: Well, I think all that writing and all that rhyming just wore her out.

NARRATOR: You mean . . . .

KID #3: Right again, oh most intelligent one.

KID #2: You see, the old lady is getting on in years. She's just not as young as she once was. And all that writing and rhyming took a lot out of her. You know how it is with writers!

NARRATOR: So, what will happen now?

KID #3: We're not sure. But one thing's for sure. We're not planning to stay around here and listen to that racket for the rest of our lives.

NARRATOR: So, what *are* you going to do?

KID #1: I think we'll just pack our bags and leave this town for a while. We'll let the old lady snore her heart out. After she wakes up in a couple of days, maybe we'll come back. Until then, let the squirrels and chipmunks and bears listen to her.

NARRATOR: So, that's it? She spends her whole life writing and rhyming and rhyming and writing and this is all the thanks she gets?

KID #3:	Hey, don't blame us. It's just that we can't take all that racket. It's really driving us nuts!
NARRATOR:	OK. See you around.
KID #1:	Yeah, see you.
KID #3:	Yeah, bye.
KID #2:	*(softly)* One, two, buckle my shoe. Three, four . . . .
KID #3:	Now cut that out!

Mary Had a Little Lamb
That Made a Big "No-No"
on the Classroom Floor

STAGING: All of the characters can be standing or sitting on stools, except for the lamb, who can be walking around as the story is being told. The narrator should be seated on a tall stool.

Narrator
X

Mary
X

Lamb
X

Teacher
X

Billy
X

Sally
X

José
X

NARRATOR:	Mary had a little lamb,
	Its fleece was white as snow;
	And everywhere that Mary went,
	The lamb was sure to go.
	It followed her to school one day,
	That was against the rule;
	It made the children laugh and play
	To see a lamb at school.
BILLY:	Hey, Mary, how come you brought your lamb to school today?
MARY:	I couldn't find anybody to take care of it. Both of my parents are working, and my grandmother is in Florida. I couldn't leave it alone.
SALLY:	Why didn't you just leave it in your yard?

MARY:	It gets lonely whenever I leave. Then, it starts getting sad.
JOSÉ:	All right! Now we'll have enough players for a game of kickball at recess. Does your lamb know how to play?
MARY:	I don't know, but we can teach it.
LAMB:	Baaaaa, baaaaa, baaaaa.
TEACHER:	Mary, why do you have that lamb at school? Don't you know the rule?
MARY:	Yes, Teacher, I know the rule. But I couldn't leave it at home.
TEACHER:	I'm sorry, Mary, but rules are rules. You won't be able to keep that lamb here. You'll have to take it home right after math class.
NARRATOR:	The boys and girls are all doing their math. Then something terrible happens in the classroom.
SALLY:	Wow! What's that smell?
BILLY:	Whew! Does it stink in here!
JOSÉ:	Ooooo-weeee! Somebody open the windows!
TEACHER:	Mary, did your lamb just do something?
MARY:	Gee, I don't know, Teacher. *(she turns to look at the lamb)* Oh, Lamby-Poo, what did you do? Oh, no, it's all over the floor.
TEACHER:	*(angrily)* Mary, get that lamb out of here now. Clean up that floor. You're in big trouble, young lady. I'm calling your parents.

MARY: I'm sorry, Teacher. I'll clean it up right now. I'll never bring my lamb to school again.

NARRATOR: Mary had a little lamb,
Its fleece was white as snow.
But in the classroom one bright day
The lamb just had to go.
It made a mess upon the floor,
So bad I cannot tell.
And all the children had to leave
They couldn't stand the smell.

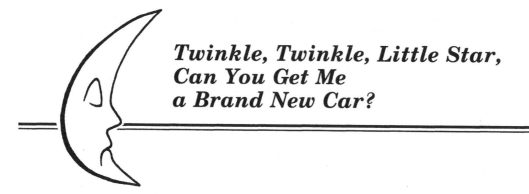

Twinkle, Twinkle, Little Star, Can You Get Me a Brand New Car?

STAGING: The "star" should be in the far corner of the staging area. Harold should be standing and shouting or talking in a loud voice to the star. The narrator can be seated on a stool or chair.

Star
X

Harold
X

Narrator
X

NARRATOR: Once upon a time, there was this star. Its name was Twinkle Twinkle Little Star. I know, that's a really silly name for a star, but that's what they used to call it. Anyway, kids around the world would see this star and make wishes to it. Let's listen in on one of those wishes.

HAROLD: Twinkle Twinkle Little Star, can you get me a brand new car?

STAR: *(indignantly)* What? A new car! Are you crazy? You're just a kid, what do you want a car for?

HAROLD: Well, I just thought I'd ask for as much as I could. You never know, I could get lucky.

STAR: Hey, look, buddy. I'm getting just a little sick and tired of all you greedy kids asking me for everything you want. Doesn't anybody work anymore?

HAROLD: Sure we do. My mother makes me take out the garbage and sweep the kitchen, and my dad makes me clean out the garage and pull up lots of weeds.

STAR: So, do you want a medal?

HAROLD: No, I just want a car.

STAR: Well, you're out of luck, buddy, because all the requests for cars are filled. Come back in a couple of years when you're old enough to drive.

HAROLD: Well, then what can I wish for?

STAR: I don't know, that's up to you.

HAROLD: Well, then can I have a train?

STAR: No, I'm all out of trains.

HAROLD: Well, then how about a brand new bicycle?

STAR: I'm afraid you're going to have to stand in line for that one, too, pal.

HAROLD: Well, how about a dog?

STAR: Hey, what do I look like, a veterinarian? I'm a star, not a pet store.

HAROLD: Can I wish for a sister?

STAR: Forget it, buddy.

HAROLD: How about lots and lots of money?

STAR: You and every other kid in the universe.

HAROLD: Well, then what can I get from you?

STAR: Not much. Let me see. *(pauses)* It looks like all I've got left are a couple of packages of brussels sprouts, a stale peanut butter sandwich, a broken alarm clock, and a snowman left over from last winter.

HAROLD: Is that it?

STAR: I'm afraid so. You see, I've been granting so many wishes lately that I'm fresh out of supplies. It's going to be a couple of years before I'm stocked up again.

HAROLD: Oh, gee!

STAR: Don't worry about it, kid. By then you'll have a job, you'll be making lots of money, and you won't need any Twinkle Twinkle Little Star to wish on.

HAROLD: *(dejectedly)* I guess you're right.

STAR: Hey, keep your chin up. There's another nursery rhyme about a magic lamp that you might want to try. Take a look at some books in your library. Maybe if you rub that lamp you'll get all your wishes. Me, I'm fresh out. Sorry.

HAROLD: Well, thanks anyway. See you around.

Little Miss Muffet
Sat on a Tuffet
and Squashed a Poor Little Spider

STAGING: The narrator stands at a podium. Miss Muffet should sit in a chair. The other characters should all be standing and should approach Miss Muffet when it is their turn to speak. Note that the audience has a part at the end.

	Cat	*Dog*	*Chicken*	*Hamster*
	X	X	X	X

Miss Muffet
X

Narrator
X

Audience

X X X X X
X X X X X X X X X

NARRATOR: Once there was this person who ate breakfast in the forest. Everybody called her Little Miss Muffet (even though she was seven feet tall and 114 years old). She used to sit around all morning eating bowls of oatmeal, scrambled eggs, and other mushy things. She also ate curds and whey—which taste like fried dog food and brussels sprouts. One morning, while she was eating, some animals stopped by to see her.

MISS MUFFET: *(insistently)* Hey, look, guys, all I want to do is just sit here and eat my measly breakfast in peace and quiet. I don't bother you . . . you don't bother me. OK?

CAT:	I'd sure like to taste that stuff in your bowl, Muffet lady. All I get to eat is soggy cat food and dead mice. Some curds and whey would be great just about now.
MISS MUFFET:	*(angrily)* Hey, bug off! Just let me eat my breakfast by myself.
DOG:	Wow, you sure are grouchy! You think you've got it rough. How about me? All I get to eat is old horse-meat and table scraps. I don't know about you, but I've just about had it.
MISS MUFFET:	*(defiantly)* You know, you guys are beginning to get on my nerves. Don't you have something better to do than bother me?
NARRATOR:	It seems that Miss Muffet is beginning to get a little angry. Let's listen some more to see what she does.
CHICKEN:	*(happily)* Hey, good-looking, can you share some of that stuff with me? You know, it's not easy living on a diet of worms and birdseed. I could go for some real food.
MISS MUFFET:	*(more angrily)* Why don't you all just take a hike! You're really starting to bother me. Just leave me alone! OK?
HAMSTER:	*(meekly)* Please, oh, please. Just one tiny little bite?
MISS MUFFET:	*(standing up)* That does it! The next one who comes along and bothers me is going to get it . . . *(shaking her fist)* and I'm not kidding! *(she sits down)*
NARRATOR:	S-Q-U-I-S-H! S-Q-U-I-S-H! S-Q-U-I-S-H!

AUDIENCE: O-O-O-O-O-O-O-O-O, GROSS!

NARRATOR: S—Q—U—I—S—H! S—Q—U—I—S—H! S—Q—U—I—S—H!

AUDIENCE: O—O—O—O—O—O—O—O—O, REALLY GROSS!

NARRATOR: And so it was that Miss Muffet sat down on a poor little spider who was just passing by. Of course, the spider was smushed and smashed and squashed all over the place. The other animals got sick to their stomachs and left the forest. And they never bothered Miss Muffet again.

Old Mother Hubbard
Went to the Cupboard
and Got Sick at What She Saw

STAGING: The narrators can sit on stools or chairs to the front and side of the characters. The characters can stand or sit in chairs. Note that the audience has a part at the end.

Old Mother Hubbard
X

Icky Slimy Thing
X

Dog
X

Narrator #1
X

Narrator #2
X

Audience

X X X X X
X X X X X X X
X X X X X X X X

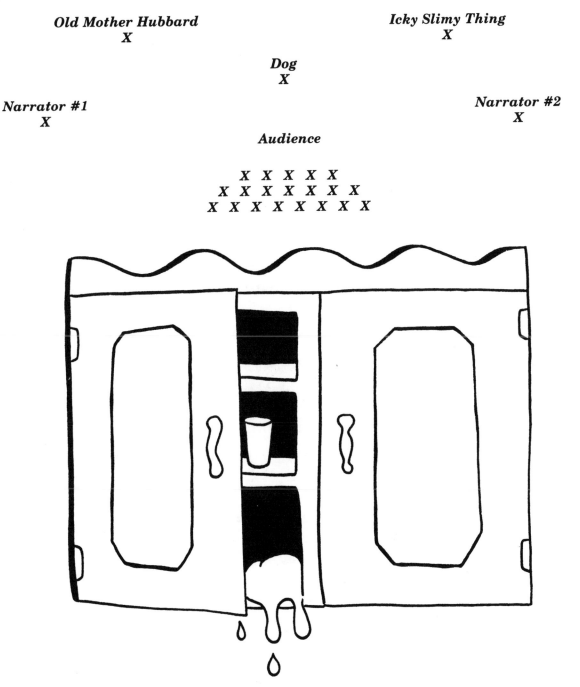

NARRATOR #1:   Old Mother Hubbard
Went to the cupboard
To give her poor dog a bone;
But when she got there,
She opened the door,
And a great big icky slimy thing fell on the floor.

OLD MOTHER HUBBARD: Oooooooooo, Uuuuuggggg, G-R-O-S-S. What is that thing?

DOG: That's the grossest thing I've ever seen. What did you put in there?

OLD MOTHER HUBBARD: Nothing. Nothing at all. I just keep dog food, a couple of bottles of catsup, and a few containers of yogurt in there.

DOG: Hey Mother H., haven't you ever heard of a refrigerator? Your yogurt has turned into one of the grossest, ickiest, and slimiest things in the universe.

OLD MOTHER HUBBARD: What's your beef? At least you're getting something to eat.

DOG: If you think I'm going to eat that thing, then you've got another thing coming. I'd rather chew on somebody's shoe.

OLD MOTHER HUBBARD: That can be arranged.

NARRATOR #2: Unfortunately, there was nothing left in the house to feed the dog. So the dog went to bed hungry. That night, while he and Old Mother Hubbard were sleeping, the great big icky slimy thing began to grow. And grow. And grow. And it turned into an enormous icky slimy thing that ate up everything in its path.

ICKY SLIMY THING: Hey, don't blame me. I've got to eat, too.

NARRATOR #1: Soon the icky slimy thing was eating up everything in the house—even Old Mother Hubbard and the dog. It was getting bigger and bigger.

NARRATOR #2: Just then, the Big Bad Wolf wandered over from the Three Little Pigs story because he thought Old Mother Hubbard's house belonged to one of the pigs. He stuck his head in the door to see if any of the pigs were home. That's when the icky slimy thing grabbed him and ate him up.

NARRATOR #1: I guess that means that this is the end of the story.

NARRATOR #2: And it's also the end of the wolf.

AUDIENCE: Yea! Yea! Yea!

Hey, Diddle, Diddle, the Cat and the Fiddle, the Cow Just Can't Get over the Moon

---

STAGING: The narrator stands at a lectern or podium. Each of the other characters can stand in a loose semicircle or sit on chairs.

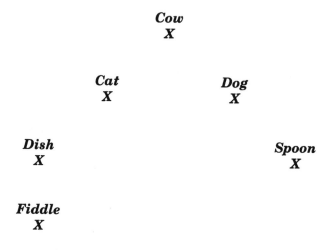

                                        Cow
                                          X

                        Cat   *Dog*
                          X   X

              Dish   *Spoon*
                X   X

        Fiddle
           X

  Narrator
      X

NARRATOR: Once upon a time there was this cow. The cow was part of a well-known Mother Goose story. You've probably heard it. It goes something like this: Hey, diddle, diddle, the cat and the fiddle, the cow jumped over the moon, and so on, and so on, and so on. Well, to tell the truth, the cow really didn't jump over the moon. Let's listen and find out why.

COW: Hey, guys, we've got a real problem. Someone is going to write a Mother Goose rhyme about us, and for it to rhyme, they're going to have me jump over the moon. I mean, can you believe that?

FIDDLE:	That's unbelievable, Cow. Why would they want you to jump all the way over the moon?
COW:	Well, actually they needed a word that would rhyme with *spoon*.
SPOON:	Hey, now, don't blame me. I'm just going to run away with the dish.
DISH:	Yeah, that's right. But, you see, these writers couldn't figure out any words that would rhyme with *dish* except for *wish* and *fish*. And I know they don't want anyone running away with a fish.
SPOON:	That's why they had to put me at the end of that line.
DOG:	Yeah, they sure couldn't put me at the end of a line. What would I rhyme with? *Hog? Frog? Jog?*
FIDDLE:	That's right. Dog is just supposed to laugh in this story. It would change everything if he and a frog ran away.
CAT:	Hey, wait a minute. How is a dish able to talk?
DISH:	Don't worry about it. This is just a Mother Goose rhyme. All kinds of things, from plates to pancakes, can talk in these stories. Don't let it bother you.
CAT:	OK.
COW:	Now, wait a second, guys. We're getting away from my problem, which is, how am I going to be able to soar over the moon? I'm not a space shuttle, you know, and I'm not the lightest animal in the world. So what do I do?

SPOON: Maybe we could invent some kind of rocket launcher to get you up in space.

COW: Do we look like rocket scientists? How are we going to invent a rocket launcher?

DOG: Well, we can talk, so we must be pretty smart.

DISH: Yeah, but not smart enough to get fat old Bossy here up into space and up and over the moon.

CAT: So what are we going to do?

COW: I guess we are just going to have to let the writer use his imagination to get me over the moon and back safely so that I can rhyme with my friend the spoon.

NARRATOR: And so it was. The cow was just too fat to get over the moon in real life. But the writer made up a real neat poem that made you think that the cow could actually jump that high. And this is what he wrote:

Hey, diddle, diddle, the cat and the fiddle,
The cow jumped over the moon;
The little dog laughed to see such a sport,
And the dish ran away with the spoon.

COW: Hey, thanks a lot, guys!

Rub-a-Dub Dub, How Did All Those Guys Get in That Tub?

STAGING: The two narrators sit on tall stools. The other characters should be sitting in a tight circle in the middle of the staging area. (Note: One person in the audience has a small part, too.)

<pre>
                          A Person
                             X

              F Person   B Person
                 X   X

           E Person   C Person
              X   X

                      D Person
                         X

Narrator #1   Narrator #2
    X   X
</pre>

NARRATOR 1: Rub-a-dub dub, three men in a tub. OK, OK I'd better stop there. First of all, you're probably wondering why this story has *six* people in a tub. Second, you might be wondering why all those people would want to take a bath together in the first place. Hey, don't ask me those tough questions—I'm just telling this story. Why don't you ask them? *(points to the characters)*.

PERSON A: Hey, guys, who decided that we should all take a bath together?

PERSON B: Don't look at me!

PERSON C:	It wasn't my idea.
PERSON D:	Frankly, I think we're all just a little bit crazy.
PERSON E:	Hey, who are you calling crazy?
PERSON F:	What I don't understand is why we're all taking a bath with our clothes still on.
PERSON A:	Hey, you know, you're right. I *do* have my clothes on.
PERSON B:	We must be some of the silliest story characters around. What will people think of us now?
PERSON C:	Well, to be honest, they probably think we're not too bright.
PERSON D:	*(pointing to audience)* Look at them staring at us. They must think we're dumber than dirt.

PERSON E:	*(pointing to an individual in the audience)* Hey, you, why are you staring at me?
AUDIENCE INDIVIDUAL:	Because I think you're dumber than dirt.
PERSON F:	Hey, you two, just cut it out.
PERSON A:	Look, guys, I think we have another problem.
PERSON B:	What's that?
PERSON A:	How are we all going to get clean if there's so many of us in this tub?
PERSON C:	You know, you're right. I mean, when I take a bath at home it's just me and my rubber ducky.
PERSON D:	Ha, Ha, Ha. You mean to tell me that you have a rubber ducky?
PERSON C:	That's right. So what?!
PERSON E:	Knock it off. I have a rubber ducky, too. And so do they. *(points to Person A and Person F)* Lots of people have rubber duckies.
PERSON F:	Hey! Let's get back to our original problem. How are we going to get clean with all of us in this tub?
PERSON B:	To be honest, I don't think that's our original problem. I think our problem is going to be how we're all going to get *out* of this tub.
PERSON C:	You know what, guys? I think we have more problems than we know what to do with. Maybe we should get the writer to help us out. *(points to Narrator 1)* Hey, Narrator, do you think the writer could help us out? What happened to him?

NARRATOR 1: Don't ask me. All I'm doing is getting this stupid story started. It's up to you guys to finish it.

NARRATOR 2: And so it was. A whole bunch of people, with their clothes still on, got into a teeny tiny tub to take a bath. They didn't know how they got there, and they didn't know how they were going to get out of there. It was really sad. But the saddest part was that nobody could find the writer—the one person who could get them all out of this story. So they all just sat there in the tub . . . rub-a-dub dub . . . rub-a-dub dub!

Note: This story can end right here. Or, you may wish to use it as an unfinished story and invite students to contribute their own possible endings.

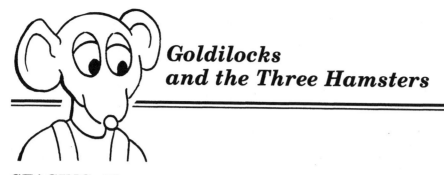

Goldilocks and the Three Hamsters

STAGING: The narrator sits off to the side on a tall stool or chair. The other characters can be standing or sitting in chairs.

Papa Hamster
X

Baby Hamster
X

Mama Hamster
X

Goldilocks
X

Narrator
X

NARRATOR: Once upon a time, there were three hamsters. One was Baby Hamster, and he was the smallest. The middle-sized hamster was Mama Hamster. And, of course, the biggest hamster was Papa Hamster. They all lived together in a cage in Mrs. Johnson's classroom. One day, Mama Hamster baked some hamster food in the hamster oven and put it on the hamster table for breakfast. They all sat around to eat.

BABY HAMSTER: Owwww! This hamster food is too hot!

MAMA HAMSTER: You are right, Baby Hamster. What shall we do until it is cool?

PAPA HAMSTER: Let's go for a run on our exercise wheel. When we get done running around and around and around, the hamster food will be just right.

NARRATOR: The hamster family left their hamster breakfast cooling on the hamster table. They walked over to the exercise wheel on the other side of their hamster cage to go for a morning run. While they were on the wheel, a little girl named Goldilocks, who was a student in Mrs. Johnson's class, walked by the cage. She was on her way to get her pencil sharpened. As she passed, she smelled the hamster food.

GOLDILOCKS: Ooohhh. That hamster food smells so good. I didn't have anything for breakfast and I'm really hungry. Maybe I'll just take a quick peek inside this cage.

NARRATOR: Goldilocks looked through the bars of the cage and into the hamster house. She opened the cage door and stuck her head right inside.

GOLDILOCKS: Look at this great big bowl of hamster food. I'll have to try it. Oh, no, this is just too hot! Maybe I'll eat this middle-sized bowl. No, it is just a little too cold! I'll try this tiny bowl. Oh, yes! This is just right!

NARRATOR: Goldilocks ate all of the hamster food in Baby Hamster's bowl. Then she began to look around the inside of the hamster house. She noticed the three hollow tubes that the hamsters played in.

GOLDILOCKS: Look at those tubes. I think I'll stick my finger in the big one. Goodness! This one's too big. Maybe the middle-sized tube is better. No, it's still too big. I think this little one will be just right.

NARRATOR: But when Goldilocks put her big, fat finger inside the tiny, little tube, it got stuck. She shook and shook and shook her finger until the tube flew off and smashed into a hundred pieces on the floor. That made her very angry and very upset. She decided to look around the house some more. She found the three water bottles that the hamsters used to get their drinks.

GOLDILOCKS: Those water bottles sure do look interesting. I think I'll try them. I'll try the big one first. Oh, no, this is much too big for me. Perhaps the middle-sized one is better. No, this one's not right either. I'll try the little one. Yes, this one is just the right size. I'll use it to get a drink of water.

NARRATOR:	Goldilocks tried to pull her head out of the cage. Unfortunately, her big head got stuck in the bars. Soon, the three hamsters came back from their exercise wheels.
BABY HAMSTER:	Look, Papa! Somebody has been in our house.
MAMA HAMSTER:	Let's go in very carefully and very slowly.
PAPA HAMSTER:	SOMEONE HAS BEEN EATING MY HAMSTER FOOD!
MAMA HAMSTER:	SOMEONE HAS BEEN EATING MY HAMSTER FOOD!
BABY HAMSTER:	SOMEONE HAS BEEN EATING MY HAMSTER FOOD! And it's all gone!
NARRATOR:	The hamsters began looking around the house. Papa Hamster saw that his hollow tube had been moved.
PAPA HAMSTER:	SOMEONE HAS BEEN PLAYING WITH MY HOLLOW TUBE!
MAMA HAMSTER:	SOMEONE HAS BEEN PLAYING WITH MY HOLLOW TUBE!
BABY HAMSTER:	SOMEONE HAS BEEN PLAYING WITH MY HOLLOW TUBE! And they broke it into a thousand pieces.
NARRATOR:	The hamsters kept walking around the inside of their house. Papa Hamster was the first to see that his water bottle had been disturbed.

PAPA HAMSTER: SOMEONE HAS BEEN MESSING WITH MY WATER BOTTLE!

MAMA HAMSTER: SOMEONE HAS BEEN MESSING WITH MY WATER BOTTLE!

BABY HAMSTER: SOMEONE HAS BEEN MESSING WITH MY WATER BOTTLE! And, look, there she is with her head caught in our cage.

NARRATOR: *(faster and faster)* Goldilocks got very scared. The three hamsters began running toward her. Goldilocks pulled harder and harder. The hamsters were getting closer and closer. Goldilocks was getting more and more scared. Finally, with one last yank she pulled her head out just in the nick of time. *(slowly)* After that, she promised she would never, ever eat hamster food again. The three hamsters got a large rat to guard their house and put locks on all their doors. And they all lived happily ever after.

The Big Bad Pig
and the Three Little Wolves

Staging: The narrator sits on a tall stool. The three wolves and the pig should be standing.

Third Little Wolf
X

Second Little Wolf
X

First Little Wolf
X

Big Bad Pig
X

Narrator
X

NARRATOR: Everybody's heard the story about the three little pigs and their three little houses. But have you ever heard the story about the three little wolves? Well, in this story the three little wolves leave home and begin walking in the woods. Then, something really terrible happens.

FIRST LITTLE WOLF: Hey, brothers, it looks like we're lost in the woods.

SECOND LITTLE WOLF: You're right. I guess we had better all build a house for the night.

THIRD LITTLE WOLF: OK, let's get started.

NARRATOR: Each of the wolves goes off to hunt for materials. Now, you should know that two of the three little wolves are not as smart as your everyday average wolf. In fact, they're about as dumb as a wolf can get. Listen, and you'll see for yourself.

FIRST LITTLE WOLF: I'm going to build a nice three-story house out of these weeds I found by the river.

SECOND LITTLE WOLF: Are you crazy? Do you know what can happen? A big, bad pig could come along and blow your house down.

THIRD LITTLE WOLF: Well, little brother, what are you going to use to build your house?

SECOND LITTLE WOLF: I found thousands and thousands of dried leaves in the forest. I'm going to use them to build an enormous house in the middle of the forest.

FIRST LITTLE WOLF: You know, you must be just as crazy as I am. Don't you know that that big, ugly, terrible pig with his incredibly bad breath could just as easily come along and blow your house down, too?

SECOND LITTLE WOLF: Gosh, maybe you're right. *(turning to the Third Little Wolf)* What are you going to do, brother?

THIRD LITTLE WOLF: I think I'm going to get out of these woods and move to a 12-story apartment building in the city. That will keep that big, lard-faced, funny-nosed, overweight porker from blowing down my house. How would you guys like to move in with me?

BIG BAD PIG: Hey, wait a minute. This isn't how the story is supposed to turn out.

NARRATOR: *(standing)* Well, guess what, Pork Breath? We just decided to change this story right in the middle. I guess you're just left out.

BIG BAD PIG: Well, now what am I supposed to do?

NARRATOR: I guess you'll just have to find yourself another story. Why don't you go over to Little Red Riding Hood and her grandmother's house? Maybe she'll invite you over for dinner. Maybe she'll even have *you* for dinner. Yum, yum, pork chops for dinner with lots of gravy and mashed potatoes. Maybe we'll even have you for dinner. Doesn't that sound good, boys?

FIRST LITTLE WOLF:	Yum, yum. That does sound good.
SECOND LITTLE WOLF:	Ummmmmmmmmmm!
THIRD LITTLE WOLF:	Yummmmmmmmmm!
BIG BAD PIG:	Hey, stop looking at me that way, you guys. This isn't the way the story is supposed to turn out. The writer was supposed to make me big and bad, not the other way around. Anyway, what did I ever do to you? *(backing away as the Narrator and the three wolves begin approaching)* Hey, boys, just get away. Now stop it! No, no, no!!! *(exits rapidly off stage with the others in pursuit)*

Humpty Dumpty Cracks Up
(Film at 11:00)

STAGING: The narrator should be sitting on a tall stool near the front center of the staging area. The other characters should be standing.

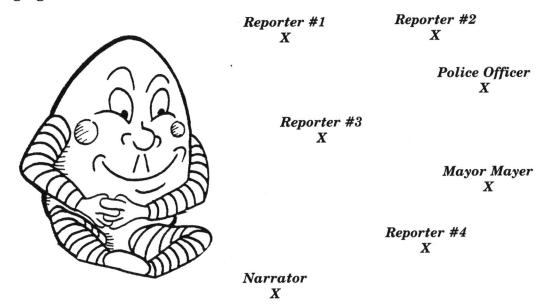

	Reporter #1 X	Reporter #2 X
		Police Officer X
	Reporter #3 X	
		Mayor Mayer X
	Reporter #4 X	
Narrator X		

NARRATOR: Once upon a time there were these three bears who....

REPORTER #1: *(interrupting)* Excuse me, buddy. But this just came in. We take you now to a wall just outside of town for this late-breaking story. Come in, Reporter #2.

REPORTER #2 Thanks, Reporter #1. We're standing here by this wall just outside the town. It's the site of a horrible, terrible accident. Let's talk to the police officer from the City Police. Tell us, Officer, what happened here?

POLICE OFFICER: Well, it seems that this big, round guy climbed to the top of the wall. Nobody knows why he did it. To be honest, I think he was a little cracked to begin with.

REPORTER #2:   Well, then what happened?

POLICE OFFICER: Just as he was sitting there . . . we're not sure how it happened . . . maybe it was a gust of wind or he just lost his balance or he wasn't paying attention . . . .

REPORTER #2:   What was it? What was it?

POLICE OFFICER: Well, for some reason, he just fell off the wall and splattered all over the sidewalk. His brains were scrambled all over the place. Runny stuff poured out of him. And there were pieces of him scattered in all directions.

REPORTER #1: *(excitedly)* Thanks, Reporter #2. We're going to have to break away. This just came into the newsroom. It seems that the mayor is about to make a speech. We take you now, live, to city hall, where Reporter #3 is standing by. Come in, Reporter #3.

REPORTER #3: We're standing here just outside city hall, where Mayor Mayer is about to address the . . . . Oh, here comes the mayor now, let's listen in.

MAYOR MAYER: *(officially)* My fellow citizens, we have a great tragedy on our hands. It seems as though a big, round character has just fallen off the town wall. We have police there now and should have an update for you shortly. There is no reason to panic.

REPORTER #4: Excuse me, Mayor Mayer, but what is being done about this situation?

MAYOR MAYER: We have called all the king's horses and all the king's men. We hope to have him back together again.

REPORTER #4: Do you have any leads? Are there any breaks in the case?

MAYOR MAYER: At this moment, no. But we will work day and night on this matter until it is cleaned up.

REPORTER #1:   Well, there you have it folks; the latest update. As soon as something else breaks, we'll have the information to you immediately. We now return you to our regularly scheduled program.

Peter Piper Picked a Peck of Pickled Peppers That Made Everybody Really Sick to Their Stomachs

STAGING: There is no narrator for this story, nor do any of the characters have a name (they are simply designated by numbers). The characters can stand around in a loose circle or sit on chairs in a semicircle facing the audience.

```
              #3           #4
              X            X

        #2                      #5
        X                       X

   #1                              #6
   X                               X
```

#1:   Peter Piper picked a peck

#2:   Of pickled peppers;

#3:   A peck of pickled peppers

#4:   Peter Piper picked.

#1:   If Peter Piper picked a peck

#2:   Of pickled peppers,

#3:   Where's the peck of pickled peppers

#4:   Peter Piper picked?

#5:   Hey, what if Peter Piper planted a patch of peppered pickles?

#6:　Well, then he would have to peek at a pair of planted poppers.

#1:　Are you sure he wouldn't plug a plot of plastic pockets?

#2:　Of course. He's just not the type to permit a peep at peeling paper.

#3:　But what if Peter Piper pinched a part of pastel pastries?

#4:　Then he would have to pick his peck of pickled peppers with a pair of purple pleated parts.

#5:　Or put a pot of partly priced potatoes in a peck of private produce.

#6:　And then the peck of pickled peppers would be packaged with the poppies Peter Piper punched and pulled and pushed.

#1:　And the peck of pickled peppers would make Peter Piper pooped.

[Repeat again at a faster pace]

Jack and Jill Don't Understand Why They Have to Go up and down a Hill

STAGING: The narrator is seated on a tall stool. The characters can be standing or seated on tall stools.

Jack
X

Jill
X

Narrator
X

NARRATOR: Once upon a time there were these two kids, Jack and Jill. They would spend all day going up this hill, but they never understood why. They never knew what they were supposed to do (I guess they never read the original story). Let's listen in on one of their conversations.

JILL: Hey, Jack. Do you know that this is the 10th time we've gone up this hill today? I still don't understand why the author has us going up this stupid hill.

JACK: Yeah. I don't understand either. Are we supposed to see something at the top of the hill? Are we supposed to get something at the top of the hill? Are we supposed to do something at the top of the hill? I just don't get it!

JILL: Well, as I see it, the author wants us to go up the hill, do something at the top of the hill, and then come back down to the bottom of the hill. I don't know about you, but that sounds like the stupidest thing I've ever heard. I'm sure getting sick and tired of this stupid, stupid hill!

JACK: I don't think it's the hill that's stupid. I think the author is stupid. Who would write a story about two kids going up and down a hill all day for no reason at all? Where's the excitement? Where's the mystery?

JILL: You're right. This story is nothing like the fairy tales and Mother Goose rhymes that kids like to read. Those stories have kids exploring deep, dark forests filled with evil stepmothers and other weird creatures that eat little children. Or they get to explore mysterious castles filled with fire-breathing dragons or enchanted princes. Or they get to talk with animals that speak perfect English. And, of course, they all have happy endings.

JACK: As you said, the author who wrote this story sure must be stupid. He didn't even put in a dragon, or a big bad wolf, or an evil giant at the top of the hill.

JILL: Maybe we should get another author for this story. Someone who can make this a really exciting story.

JACK: Yeah, you're right. Let's go.

NARRATOR: And so it was that Jack and Jill decided to go off in search of another author for their story. Of course, they didn't go up the hill like the old author wanted them to. Instead, they flew by airplane to California. There, they met a very smart author who decided to turn their story into a Hollywood movie.

Old MacDonald Had a Farm
and, Boy, Did It Stink (E-I-E-I-O)

STAGING: The narrator stands off to the side. The other characters should stand and walk around as they are speaking.

```
                                        Cow              Donkey
                                         X                 X


                              Pig                Duck
                               X                  X


                    Rooster
                      X



          Narrator
             X
```

NARRATOR: This is a true story. It's a story about a farmer named MacDonald who owned a farm—not just any farm, but a farm with real live talking animals. You should know that old MacDonald wasn't the tidiest farmer in the world. In fact, his farm really smelled. *(The narrator holds his or her nose)* Indeed, folks from seven counties around would hold their noses and go, "Ooo-Wee, that sure does smell!" But, I guess I should just let the characters standing behind me tell you the real story.

COW: WHEW! OH, WOW!! OOOOOO-WEEEEE!!! This place really stinks. I means *stinks* with a capital *S*!

DONKEY: Yeah, you're not kidding. This has got to be the smelliest barnyard in seven counties; no, make that seven countries! It stinks so much that the paint is peeling off the barn and the glass in the windows is melting. It's like we're all living in one giant pigpen.

PIG: Hey, just wait a minute! What are you calling a pigpen? Just because me and my brothers roll around in the mud, and get dirt all over our faces, and look like great big slobs doesn't mean that we smell. How about you? All you do is stand around all day refusing to work and going, "Hee-haw, hee-haw, hee-haw."

DONKEY: Well, at least my Hee-haws don't smell. But your Oink-oinks sure do! And what about Cow? Don't you think her Moo-moos smell a lot? Maybe that's the problem. There's just too many Oink-oinks, Moo-moos, and Quack-quacks all over the place stinking it up.

DUCK: Hey, don't blame me. I just waddle around in a pond and chase after frogs. I didn't make this mess. I just live here. What about Mr. Cock-a-Doodle-Doo over there?

ROOSTER: Hey, Who are you calling a cock-a-doodle-doo? Sure, I make a lot of noise and flap my wings and walk around a lot, but most of this isn't mine. What about Mr. Hee-Haw Donkey? He sure seems to be making a lot of messes around here lately. And I don't see him cleaning up any of them. You know, he's to blame for part of this smell, too.

DONKEY: Now look. I think we're all to blame here. Every one of us makes a mess somewhere in this barnyard, and we never clean it up. Frankly, the place just stinks to high heaven. It's gotten so bad that even Mrs. Old MacDonald doesn't come out of the house anymore to collect the eggs or feed the horses. We've got to do something, and we've got to do it fast.

ALL ANIMALS: *(mumbling in the background)*

NARRATOR: The animals all agreed that the barnyard was really a smelly, stinky place. But, because they weren't very bright and didn't know how to use shovels, the barnyard just got smellier and smellier. Eventually, the smell became so great that Mr. and Mrs. Old MacDonald had to move off the farm and into an apartment building in town. And that's the end of the story E-I-E-I-O.

Don't Kiss Sleeping Beauty, She's Got Really Bad Breath

STAGING: The narrator stands off to the side. The characters can each sit on a separate stool or chair, or they can stand in a circle in front of the audience.

Narrator
X

       Prince #1   *Prince #2*   *Prince #3*   *Prince #4*
         X   X   X   X

NARRATOR: Once upon a time, there was this very beautiful princess that all the princes wanted to marry. However, one day, a wicked witch made this beautiful girl eat a poisoned apple. Sleeping Beauty (that was her name) fell fast asleep. All of the princes knew that it would take a kiss to wake her up.

PRINCE #1: Wow! All I have to do is kiss Sleeping Beauty and she will awaken from her sleep to be my bride.

NARRATOR: *(to the prince)* That's right, Prince #1. *(The other Princes nod their heads in agreement)*

NARRATOR: *(to the audience)* Let's see what happens when Prince #1 returns to the castle to tell his prince friends about his discovery.

PRINCE #1: Hey, guys. You're not going to believe this, but Sleeping Beauty is sound asleep in her house in the enchanted forest. And she is waiting for one of us to give her a kiss that will wake her up.

PRINCE #2:   Well, why didn't you kiss her?

PRINCE #1:   Well . . . I don't know how to say this . . . She has really bad breath. I mean *really* bad breath! Whew! Did it stink!!!

PRINCE #3:   You mean, you didn't kiss her after all?

PRINCE #1:   No way, José. Her breath was so bad I couldn't even get in the room to get near her.

PRINCE #4:   That's hard to believe. You mean, her breath is so bad that we can't even get close enough to kiss her? Wow, what a waste that is!

PRINCE #1:   Yeah, and you know what else? She snores like a bear in hibernation. Every time she breathes, the windows rattle and dishes in her kitchen crack and break.

PRINCE #3:   Boy, that's really unbelievable!

PRINCE #1:   Not only is she stinking up the air, but she's shaking the whole neighborhood with her incredibly loud snoring. It's so bad that nobody wants to live in the enchanted forest anymore.

PRINCE #2:   Well, how are we going to wake her up? Doesn't somebody have to kiss her for this story to end the right way? Isn't that what the writer wants?

PRINCE #1:   Hey, maybe you, pal . . . but not me! If you want to go ahead and kiss old "Hog's Breath," then help yourself.

NARRATOR: And so nobody wanted to kiss Sleeping Beauty. She just slept in the forest making loud noises and stinking up the air. If you ever go into the forest and listen real hard, you can still hear her today. Just don't forget to hold your nose.

Rock-a-Bye Baby, on the Treetop— Just Be Careful or You Might Fall on Your "You Know What"

STAGING: The narrator can sit on a stool or stand. The other characters can stand or sit on tall stools. Note that the audience has a small part at the end.

                                                    Bird #1   *Bird #2*
                                                       X   X

                                                              Squirrel
                                                                 X

                                                        Baby
                                                          X

    Narrator
       X

                        Audience
                      X X X X X
                    X X X X X X X

NARRATOR: *(in a singsongy voice)* Rock-a-bye, baby, on the tree-top; When the wind blows, the cradle will rock; When the bough br . . . .

BIRD #1: Hey, just one minute. What's a baby doing up in our tree?

BIRD #2: Yeah, how did this kid get all the way up here in our branches? We were here first, you know!

BIRD #1: And how did this cradle get up here, too? I mean, did it just fly up here, did someone throw it up here, or did it just appear out of thin air?

BIRD #2:   Yeah, it just doesn't make sense. I mean, does the writer of this story think that we're nothing but a couple of dodo birds? Does he even realize that we were the ones who invented flying in the first place? Who's going to believe that a cradle just magically appeared in the branches of their local maple tree?

BABY: Waaaaaaa, waaaaaaa, waaaaaaa.

SQUIRREL: Hey, now look what you guys have done. You've upset this poor little baby.

BIRD #2:   Hey, back off, buddy. Who invited you to this little discussion? I mean, after all, all you do is gather nuts, store them in the trunk of this tree, and sleep all winter. What do you know?

SQUIRREL: Look, I was just trying to help out.

BABY: *(louder)* Waaaaaaa, waaaaaaa, waaaaaaa.

BIRD #1:   Now, he's really upset. And I'm upset. And everybody else is upset. How did we get into this mess, anyway?

BIRD #2:   I'm not sure, and I still don't understand why the writer would want to have a baby and his stupid cradle up in the branches of some old tree. It just doesn't make sense.

NARRATOR: The birds and the squirrel didn't realize it, but they had all been standing on the same branch that was holding the cradle. It wasn't long before the branch began to sag and start to break. Of course, the cradle fell out of the tree and the baby fell to the ground right on his "you know what."

AUDIENCE: *(singsongy)* When the bough breaks, the cradle will fall; Down will come baby, cradle and all.

BABY: Waaaaaaa, waaaaaaa, waaaaaaa.

Here We Go Round the Mulberry Bush and I'm Sure Getting Dizzy

STAGING: Throughout the story the narrator walks continuously in a circle around the other characters. The other characters can all be seated or standing. They should occasionally turn their heads, looking at the narrator while speaking their parts.

NARRATOR:	Here we go round the mulberry bush, the mulberry bush, the mulberry bush. Here we go round the mulberry bush so early in the . . . . Whoa, now just wait a doggone minute here. Why the heck am I spending the entire story walking around and around in circles?
KIM:	Well, I guess it's because you're the hero of this story.
NARRATOR:	If I'm the hero, then I'm one very dizzy hero.
KAREN:	To be honest, I think you were pretty dizzy to begin with.
NARRATOR:	Hey, who are you calling dizzy?
KYLE:	Hold on, guys. I think there's a real problem here.
KEN:	What do you mean?
KYLE:	Well, just look at our friendly neighborhood narrator. Ever since this story began, all he's been doing is walking around in circles.
NARRATOR:	I can't help it. I'm supposed to swing around and around some stupid mulberry bush. The only problem is, I have no idea what a mulberry bush is or what one looks like.
KIM:	Don't look at me. I've never seen one either.
KAREN:	I think I saw one in another story, but I'm not quite sure.
KEN:	What other story would that be?
KAREN:	I can't remember. But I think it had something to do with a bunch of pigs and a wolf with bad breath.

KYLE: No, it wasn't that story. I think it was the one about the silly cow who wanted to high jump over the moon.

KEN: You know what, I think it was the story about the little girl who brought that lamb to school one day. The lamb did something really gross on the floor and then the teacher had to stop in the middle of her lesson to get some paper towels and clean it . . . .

NARRATOR: HOLD IT! HOLD IT! Now wait just a gosh darn minute here. While you guys are talking about some of the finer points of Mother Goose and all her crazy characters, I'm still going around and around in circles here. And there's not even a stupid mulberry bush for miles. Can't anybody stop me?

KIM: No, I guess not. *(talking to the other characters)* Hey, guys, it looks like our friendly narrator is going to have to solve this problem alone. Let's see if we can find a story where the narrator isn't going around and around. Let's go. *(all the characters get up and begin to leave)*

NARRATOR: Hey, guys, wait up. You're not just going to leave me here. Hey wait. Wait. Hey . . . . *(the narrator continues to go around in circles as his or her voice trails off)*

Part III

SWIM ON OVER . . .
HERE'S A BUNCH OF TADPOLE TALES
(or should that be "Tadpole Tails?")

The Three Little Tadpoles

STAGING: The narrator stands at a lectern or podium at the front of the staging area. The three tadpoles sit on stools or chairs. The stork stands and moves back and forth among the other characters.

Todd Tadpole   *Thad Tadpole*   *Ted Tadpole*
X   X   X

Stan Stork
X

Narrator
X

NARRATOR: Once upon a time, three tadpoles left their parents' house. They wanted to live by themselves in the swamp.

TODD TADPOLE: Hey, brothers. Let's go look for some materials to build our homes.

THAD TADPOLE: OK, Todd. What do you say, Ted?

TED TADPOLE: It's OK with me, Thad. Is it OK with you, Todd?

TODD TADPOLE: It's OK with me, Ted. And it's OK with Thad.

NARRATOR: So Todd and Ted and Thad went in search of some building materials.

TODD TADPOLE: Oh, look, there are some rotting weeds I can use to build my house.

NARRATOR: So the first tadpole built his house out of some rotting weeds. The second tadpole kept looking.

THAD TADPOLE: Oh, look, there are some rotting branches I can use to build my house.

NARRATOR: So the second tadpole built his house out of some rotting branches. The third tadpole kept looking.

TED TADPOLE: Oh, look, there is some nice thick mud I can use to build my house.

NARRATOR: So the third tadpole built his house out of some nice thick mud. Then along came the stork.

STAN STORK: I'm so hungry. I think I'll look for some nice, juicy tadpoles to eat. Hey, first little tadpole, your house is built of rotting weeds. I think I'll blow it down.

NARRATOR: And that's just what he did. He also ate Todd Tadpole.

STAN STORK: I'm still very hungry. I think I'll look for some more juicy tadpoles to eat. Hey, second little tadpole, your house is built of rotting branches. I think I'll blow it down.

NARRATOR:	And that's just what he did. He also ate Thad Tadpole.
STAN STORK:	I'm still hungry. I think I'll go look for some more juicy tadpoles to eat. Hey, third little tadpole, your house is built of nice thick mud. I think I'll blow it down.
NARRATOR:	Now you should know that this stork wasn't very smart. Because the more he huffed and the more he puffed the more he became stuck in the mud. Tadpoles from all over the swamp came and threw mud balls at the stork. They laughed at him. They called him funny names. They threw more mud at him. Finally, the stork was able to get out of the mud. He was really mad. So he went to his friend, the big bad wolf, and told him the story. And the big bad wolf made sure that those tadpoles never called anyone any names again.

The Tadpole and the Frog

STAGING: The narrator can stand off to the side of the staging area or sit on a tall stool. The other characters can form a loose semicircle or walk around as they are speaking.

Narrator
X

Tadpole   Frog
X   X

Starter
X

NARRATOR:	Once upon a time there was a tadpole and a frog. The frog, because he was older, thought he was the faster swimmer. The tadpole, because he had a long tail, thought he was the faster swimmer.
FROG:	Hey, tadpole, I'm the fastest thing around. Nobody can beat me.
TADPOLE:	I may be small, but I'm much faster than you.
FROG:	Oh, yeah? Who says?
TADPOLE:	I say.
FROG:	Well, if you think you're so fast, then why don't we race?
TADPOLE:	OK, you're on!

NARRATOR:	The frog and the tadpole agreed to race through the swamp. All of the other animals lined up to watch.
STARTER:	It is now time for the race. The winner will be the first one to cross the finish line. Frog, are you ready?
FROG:	Yes.
STARTER:	Tadpole, are you ready?
TADPOLE:	Yes.
STARTER:	Then, on your marks. Get set. Go!

NARRATOR:	Both the tadpole and the frog zoomed across the start line. The frog did his best frog kick. The tadpole flicked his tail back and forth. The tadpole began to take the lead.
FROG:	Oh, no. That little runt is going faster than me. If this keeps up, he's going to beat me.
NARRATOR:	The tadpole got farther and farther ahead. He made a turn at the old sunken log and headed back through the weeds near the shore. In a few minutes he would win. Then, he made a terrible mistake.
TADPOLE:	I think I'll just stick my head out of the water. I want to see where that silly old frog is.
NARRATOR:	The tadpole stuck his head out of the water. But right in front of him was a big blue heron. A big blue, and very hungry, heron. Quick as a wink, that tadpole became the heron's dinner.
FROG:	Hey, what's all that noise? I think I'll go see.
NARRATOR:	And that's when the frog made the same terrible mistake. And he soon became the heron's dinner. Now nobody was left to win the race. That wouldn't be much of an ending to the story, so a bunch of writers got together and made up a story about a rabbit and a turtle who raced each other. In that story, nobody got eaten. Too bad. I hear rabbit stew and turtle soup are pretty good!

The Tadpoles Get Upset, and Then They Get Really Mad, and Then They Get Really, Really Mad

STAGING: The characters can be slowly walking around the staging area while speaking their parts. The narrator should be on a tall stool off to one side.

Dave Tadpole
X

Karen Tadpole
X

John Tadpole
X

Debbie Tadpole
X

Narrator
X

NARRATOR:

It was just one of those days. A day full of sunshine. The sky was full of nice fat insects. There were lots of smells and odors coming from the swamp. And there was lots and lots of mucky mud all around. In other words, it was a perfect day! But, over in a corner of the swamp, in a shallow pool, some tadpoles were talking. And they weren't happy.

JOHN TADPOLE: Just who do those big fat frogs think they are?

DEBBIE TADPOLE: Yeah. Just because they have slimy skin and long legs doesn't mean they're the greatest creatures in the swamp.

DAVE TADPOLE: You've got that right, sister. Just because they can wrap their tongues around every insect that flies by doesn't make them cool.

KAREN TADPOLE: How true! You know, they started out as tadpoles once. But, now that they're all grown up, they think they're better than everyone else.

JOHN TADPOLE: I don't know about you guys, but I'm really mad.

DAVE TADPOLE: Yeah, me too.

KAREN TADPOLE: Who do those guys think they are? They once had funny little tails and weird mouths, too.

DEBBIE TADPOLE: Now that they're big hotshot frogs they just want to sit around on their lily pads all day and soak up the sun.

JOHN TADPOLE: They couldn't care less that we are trying to deal with some major changes in our bodies just so we can look like them.

DAVE TADPOLE: Big shots, yeah, that's what they are, big shots.

DEBBIE TADPOLE: Right, as soon as their skin turns green and their tongues get long enough to capture a few dragonflies, they don't want to bother with us.

DAVE TADPOLE:	Did you hear about the one they call Kermit? He has his own TV show, gets to star in movies, and even has books written about him. He must *really* think he's a hot shot!
JOHN TADPOLE:	Pretty soon, he's going to have his own lily pad with racing stripes.
DEBBIE TADPOLE:	But, hey guys, that's not going to happen to us, is it?
KAREN TADPOLE:	No way, José.
DEBBIE TADPOLE:	When we grow up, we're going to remember where we came from. We're going to treat everybody nice. And we're not going to move to some lily pads on the far side of the swamp.
ALL TADPOLES:	Yeah! Yeah! Yeah!
NARRATOR:	And so the tadpoles just swam around and ate small insects all day. But soon they noticed that they were losing their tails. Their voices were changing. And they were growing legs. And they became just like their parents.

Don't Kiss Us,
We're Just a Bunch of Tadpoles

STAGING: The narrator stands and may walk from tadpole to tadpole with a makeshift microphone. Each of the tadpoles sits on a stool or chair.

	Tom Tadpole X	Terry Tadpole X
	Tony Tadpole X	Trevor Tadpole X

Narrator
X

NARRATOR: We take you now to "Tadpole Town," the site of a late-breaking story. It seems as though all of the tadpoles are hopping mad. Let's interview some of them now. Excuse me, sir, would you talk with us?

TOM TADPOLE: Well, OK, but you should know that I'm just a tadpole, so I don't speak very well.

NARRATOR: Tell our viewers, sir, what all of this noise is about.

TOM TADPOLE: Well, you see, it's like this. We're just a bunch of tiny, little tadpoles trying to mind our own business. But every time a beautiful princess is in town, she thinks she has to come down to the swamp to kiss as many of us as she can. YUCK!!! Maybe she thinks that if she kisses us, one of us will turn into a magical frog or an enchanted prince or something like that.

TERRY TADPOLE: Yeah, the problem is that we don't even have lips yet; you know, we're just little tadpoles. So, how can we kiss all those princesses back?

TOM TADPOLE: The bottom line is this: We're fed up with all of these beautiful princesses who have nothing better to do with their time than smooch a bunch of innocent tadpoles down here at the swamp.

NARRATOR: How often does this happen?

TONY TADPOLE:	*(indignantly)* Too often. All we want to do is swim around the swamp, grow some long legs, and turn into fly-eating, bug-grabbing frogs. But N-O-O-O-O-O-O-O-O-O. Those silly, little girls come down here every chance they get to play kissy-face with us.
NARRATOR:	Well, how do the other tadpoles feel about it?
TREVOR TADPOLE:	*(excitedly)* We're mad as heck. I mean, why are they trying to kiss us in the first place? We are *not* enchanted frogs. We are *not* going to turn into handsome princes. And we are *not* going to move out of the swamp and into some dusty old castle.
TERRY TADPOLE:	Yeah, Trevor's right. Any time we just want to swim around in the swamp, those silly girls come down here to see if they can kiss one or two of us. Boy, that ticks me off!
TOM TADPOLE:	And to make things even worse, there's a new castle being built at the other end of the swamp. You know what that means. More princesses will be moving into the neighborhood, and, of course, more of them will be wanting to come down to the swamp to plant their fat lips on each and every one of us. That's really gross!!!
NARRATOR:	It sounds as if you guys have a real problem on your hands.

TONY TADPOLE: Boy, you said it! After all, we're just tiny, little tadpoles with short legs, funny-looking faces, and long tails. If we were real frogs, then we would be able to hop away.

TERRY TADPOLE: That's right!

NARRATOR: It doesn't sound like there's an easy solution to this problem.

TREVOR TADPOLE: You can say that again.

NARRATOR: So, what will you do in the meantime?

TOM TADPOLE: I guess we'll just have to learn how to eat flies and other disgusting bugs. I don't think those princesses will want to kiss us when our mouths are full of insects, do you?

Two Terribly Terrific Tadpoles

STAGING: The narrator can stand to the side or in back of the two major characters. The two tadpoles stand in front of the staging area.

Narrator
X

Tammy Tadpole   *Tricia Tadpole*
X   X

NARRATOR: Once upon a time there were these two tadpoles. Now, these weren't your average tadpoles. No way. These were two of the best-looking and most intelligent girl tadpoles in the entire swamp. Every time they swam by, all the boy tadpoles would try to whistle (as you know, tadpoles don't have lips, so they can't really whistle). Anyway, these two tadpoles sure did get a lot of attention.

TAMMY TADPOLE: Hi, Tricia, how are you doing?

TRICIA TADPOLE: Just great, Tammy. What's new with you?

TAMMY TADPOLE: Oh, nothing much. I was just going to swim on over to McTadpole's and get a bugburger and some french flies. You want to come along?

TRICIA TADPOLE: Sure. Let's go.

NARRATOR: The two terribly terrific tadpoles wiggle over to the nearest McTadpole's and place their order. While eating, they continue their conversation.

TAMMY TADPOLE: I don't know about you, Tricia, but I'm getting a little tired of having all those guys stare at us every time we swim by.

TRICIA TADPOLE: So am I. They just look at us and then try to whistle with their funny-looking lips.

TAMMY TADPOLE: I wish they would find something better to do than just stare at us.

TRICIA TADPOLE: I agree. I know we're good looking and all that, but come on, guys, give us a break!

TAMMY TADPOLE: Well, you do know, Tricia, that when we get older we're going to lose our good looks. We'll have warts all over our skin, our eyes will be bugging out, our skin will be slimy and slippery, we'll have big, long tongues, and we'll have those big, old, ugly flippers at the ends of our feet. Then nobody will want to look at us.

TRICIA TADPOLE: You know, you're right, Tammy. We will really be two ugly frogs. Plus, we'll be laying all of those eggs and raising all of those children and so on and so on and so on.

TAMMY TADPOLE: It sure doesn't sound like we've got a bright future ahead of us.

TRICIA TADPOLE: You know, come to think of it, it might be best if we stayed as two, terribly terrific tadpoles for as long as we can.

TAMMY TADPOLE: Yeah. Our fun time will be over soon enough.

NARRATOR: And so it was that Tammy and Tricia decided to stay as tadpoles for as long as they could. Unfortunately, Mother Nature had other plans for them.

Part IV

THIS IS THE SECTION OF THE BOOK
THAT HAS SOME UNFINISHED SCRIPTS
AND PARTIAL STORIES
FOR YOUR STUDENTS TO COMPLETE

(Pretty neat idea, huh?)

Some Other Stuff You'll Really Enjoy Reading (Honest!)

By now, many of your students are saying things like, "My teacher is the best teacher in the world!," and "I want to be a children's author when I grow up!," "Readers theatre is better than MTV!," and other wise and wonderful quotes. (Of course, because the intelligence levels of your students have increased exponentially through the constant and continuous use of the foregoing scripts, there will no doubt be a few students in your classroom who will be saying things like "A magnificent plethora of cognitive skills have been wonderfully enhanced through my active participation in these imaginative and creatively stimulating readers theatre scripts—for which I will always remember the dynamic and enthusiastic teacher who shared them with me.")

Then again, your students may be saying things like, "Hey, I *really* have to go!!!" or "Is it time for lunch (recess, snacks, playtime, dismissal) yet?" or "I'm sorry I threw up on your new skirt, Mrs. Jones," or "Hey, Mr. Davis, Billy's putting the hamster in his mouth again!"

(Isn't it interesting that this section of the book is titled Part "IV." Of course, you know what an IV is—it's what the nurse sticks into your arm at the hospital to replace lost fluids—certainly something most primary teachers need by the end of the school day . . . and certainly by the end of the week!)

But, once again, I digress. The stories in this section of the book are designed to serve as starters for your students' own readers theatre scripts. In each case, a story has been set up but not finished. Students should be encouraged to select a "story starter" and complete it using their own ideas and conclusions. Students can add to these scripts, modify them, or alter them in accordance with their own interests, logic, or warped senses of humor. You may find it appropriate for students to work on these scripts in small groups, rather than individually. Of course, there is no right or wrong way to complete any single story; students can invent their own plots or themes as they see fit. Be sure to provide sufficient opportunities for student groups to share their stories with other members of the class or with other classes in your school. You may also wish to consider videotaping these productions and reviewing them in concert with your students. Who knows, there may be a future Hollywood legend in your class ("I accept this Oscar and wish to thank the Academy and especially Mrs. Jones, my wonderful second-grade teacher, who gave me my first start in films and continues to be my lifelong inspiration. . . .").

Little Jack Horner Sat in the Corner and Pulled a Big Purple Thing out of a Pie

STAGING: There is no narrator for this story. The characters should be milling around, much as they might do at a party or other social gathering. Jack Horner should be sitting on the floor to the side of the staging area.

                                        Adam
                                          X

                          Frank   *Bonnie*
                            X   X

                          Ernie   *Carrie*
                            X   X

                                    Donald
                                       X

Jack Horner
      X

ADAM:	Hey, what's with Jack?
BONNIE:	I don't know. He's been sitting in the corner all night.
CARRIE:	What's he doing?
DONALD:	It looks like he's sticking his thumb in that Christmas pie.
ERNIE:	Why would he want to do that?
FRANK:	Maybe he thinks there's some kind of prize in there.
ADAM:	There's no prize in a pie.
BONNIE:	All he'll get is a messy thumb.

CARRIE:	And crumbs all over the floor.
DONALD:	He'll probably get his face all dirty, too.
ERNIE:	And he'll also stain his shirt.
FRANK:	Jack's weird.
ADAM:	Hey, look. He's pulling something out of the pie.
BONNIE:	Can anyone see what it is?
CARRIE:	It's big and round.
DONALD:	And it's purple.
ERNIE:	It sort of looks like a plum.
FRANK:	Are you sure?
ERNIE:	I don't know. Why don't we go over and ask him?
BONNIE:	OK, let's go.
CARRIE:	Hey, Jack, what's that on your thumb?
JACK:	Oh, you mean this purple thing?
ADAM:	Yeah, that purple thing. What is it?

POSSIBLE CONCLUSIONS

1. Jack puts in his thumb and pulls out a plum. He says, "Hey, wait a minute, this is supposed to be a cherry pie!"

2. Jack pulls a gigantic eggplant out of the pie. Then he complains to the baker.

3. The pie is actually a colony of tiny purple people eaters. They break through the crust and attack everybody.

4. Jack throws the pie at Donald. The party turns into a giant pie fight.

5. Your idea.

There Was an Old Woman Who Lived in a Shoe and, Wow, Did It Smell!!!

STAGING: The narrator stands in back and to the side of the other characters. The other characters can stand or sit on high stools.

<pre>
                                        Narrator
                                           X

                    Child #1
                       X

     Old Woman   Child #2
         X   X

                    Child #3
                       X
</pre>

NARRATOR: There was an old woman who lived in a shoe. She had so many children, she didn't know what to do.

OLD WOMAN: Well, all I could do was move into Michael Jordan's old sneaker. It was big enough to hold all 22 children. And it had plenty of room for them to play in.

CHILD #1:   Yes, but look what we've had to put up with.

CHILD #2:   Some of us have to live right under the tongue of the shoe. And you know how smelly that can get.

CHILD #3:   Yeah, and some of us live in the toe, where it's dark and damp and stinky.

CHILD #1:   Some of our brothers and sisters lived in the heel. It just got too gross and they moved out.

CHILD #2:   Don't forget about the two who lived in the laces. They got so tangled up, it took eight hours to get them untied.

CHILD #3:   I wish we could move someplace where it isn't so stinky.

OLD WOMAN: Well, what do you suggest?

POSSIBLE CONCLUSIONS

1. The Old Woman finds a pair of size 28AAA loafers. She turns them into a duplex for the whole family.

2. The entire family gets a bad case of athlete's foot all over their bodies. They have to powder themselves twice a day.

3. The family sneaks into a shoe store. They begin living in a different pair of shoes every day.

4. The family gets an agent. They sign a million dollar contract with Nike.

5. Your idea.

Little Bo-Peep Has Lost Her Sheep and All Her Lunch Money and Her Library Book and Some Other Stuff, Too

STAGING: The narrator stands in back of or to the side of the characters. The characters can be standing or seated on tall stools.

Narrator
X

Bo-Peep　　　　*Clarence*　　　　*Sheep*
X　　　　　　　X　　　　　　　X

Mr. Smart　　　　*Sheep*
X　　　　　　　X

Penny
X

NARRATOR:	Once upon a time there was this little girl named Bo-Peep. She was a nice girl, and everybody liked her. But she had this problem. She was always losing things.
MR. SMART:	All right kids, take out your homework from last night.
BO-PEEP:	*(raising her hand)* Mr. Smart, I forgot my homework. I left it on the kitchen table this morning.
MR. SMART:	*(exasperated)* Oh, not again, Bo-Peep. You've forgotten your homework twice this week. What are we going to do with you?

BO-PEEP: I'm sorry, Mr. Smart. I can't seem to remember anything. Last week I forgot my sheep.

SHEEP: Baaaaa, baaaaa, baaaaa.

MR. SMART: What do you mean, you forgot your sheep?

BO-PEEP: I was at the park with my friends. I had my sheep with me. We were having so much fun I forgot about them. When it was time to go, the sheep were gone. We looked everywhere and couldn't find them.

PENNY: That's right. I was there. We looked everywhere. We looked in the trees. We looked in the bushes. We even looked on the jungle gym. But they were all gone.

SHEEP: Baaaaa, baaaaa, baaaaa.

BO-PEEP: A couple of days ago I lost my library book. It just vanished out of my desk.

MR. SMART: Can't you hold on to anything?

BO-PEEP: It just seems that everything I touch vanishes.

MR. SMART: What are we going to do with you?

CLARENCE: I know. Why don't we tie a string around her finger. Or pin a note to her shirt or something like that.

POSSIBLE CONCLUSIONS

1. The kids tie the sheep to Bo-Peep's hand. She never loses them again.

2. Bo-Peep invents a cellular phone called "The Bo-Peeper." People can call her and tell her to remember things.

3. Bo-Peep decides to call herself Snow White and get into a new story.

4. A wicked witch changes her into a frog. She never has to worry about forgetting anything again.

5. Your idea.

Old King Cole Was a Merry Old Soul Until He Had to Do His Math Homework

STAGING: The narrator can be standing off to one side. The other characters can be on stools or can be walking around the staging area.

Old King Cole
X

Teacher Teacher
X

Mandy
X

Candy
X

Sandy
X

Narrator
X

NARRATOR:	Old King Cole was a merry old soul. And a merry old soul was he. That is, until he had to do his math homework.
OLD KING COLE:	Hey, Teacher Teacher, how come I have to do math homework. I'm a king, you know.
TEACHER TEACHER:	Yes, I know, Cole. But you haven't learned how to subtract one number from another. How are you ever going to run a kingdom if you don't know how to subtract?
OLD KING COLE:	*(pleading)* Awwwwwww, come on, Teacher Teacher. I can hire a bunch of subtractors to do all that work for me. Why should I have to know that stuff?
TEACHER TEACHER:	Because you never know when you're going to need it. What will you do when you're not king anymore? You won't be able to hire anybody then.
MANDY:	Yeah, king buddy, if someone takes over your kingdom and throws you out, you'll be on your own.
CANDY:	Besides, the new king will probably hire all of the subtractors in the land, and there won't be any left for you.
SANDY:	That means that you'll have to do all of your subtracting by yourself—with nobody to help you.
TEACHER TEACHER:	So, you see, if you don't do your math homework now, you'll never be able to retire.
OLD KING COLE:	Dang. There must be something I can do. I just hate math.

POSSIBLE CONCLUSIONS

1. Old King Cole hires all the kids in the class. He pays them lots of money to do his math homework for him.

2. Old King Cole buys a computer. He never has to worry about doing math homework again.

3. Old King Cole passes a law making math homework illegal.

4. Old King Cole practices and practices. Soon he becomes the best math student in the entire kingdom.

5. Your idea.

Peter, Peter, Pumpkin Eater, Didn't Have Much Money So He and His Family Lived Inside a Smelly Old Pumpkin

STAGING: The narrator can be seated on a chair to one side of the staging area. The other characters can be standing or seated on stools.

```
                              Citizen #1        Citizen #2
                                  X                 X

                              Citizen #3        Citizen #4
                                  X                 X

                                      Citizen #5
                                          X

     Narrator
        X
```

NARRATOR: Once upon a time there was this guy named Peter. He was too lazy to build a house for his family, so he moved them into a used pumpkin on the other side of town. It really wasn't such a bad idea. The family never starved because they could just eat the walls and nibble on the seeds they found scattered throughout the pumpkin house.

Things were fine until the pumpkin started to rot. Nasty smells would come from the pumpkin, and flies would circle the top. The citizens began to complain. They would often stop to talk to each other at the local shopping mall.

CITIZEN #1:   *(angrily)* Can you believe that Pumpkineater guy? First he moves his whole family into an old jack-'o-lantern. Then he lets it get so rotten that no one can go anywhere near it.

CITIZEN #2:   *(disgustedly)* Yeah, and I'm getting pretty sick of it. I can't even go outside and sit on my back porch anymore. The stench is just terrible.

CITIZEN #3:   Whew! Stinky! It's so bad that my hair is falling out. My toenails are starting to turn green.

CITIZEN #4:   It's a mess. I feel sorry for the kids. They're the ones who have to live in it.

CITIZEN #5:   Something has to be done.

POSSIBLE CONCLUSIONS

1. The citizens decide to make a giant pumpkin pie.

2. A swarm of flies invades the pumpkin, forcing the Pumpkineater family to move.

3. Mrs. Pumpkineater cans her house.

4. Peter is arrested for eating his own house.

5. Your idea.

The Gingerbread Boy
Gets Baked at 350 Degrees
for 15 to 20 Minutes

STAGING: The narrator can stand off to the side. The other characters can sit on tall stools or in chairs.

Narrator
X

Gingerbread Boy
X

Little Old Woman   *Little Old Man*
X   X

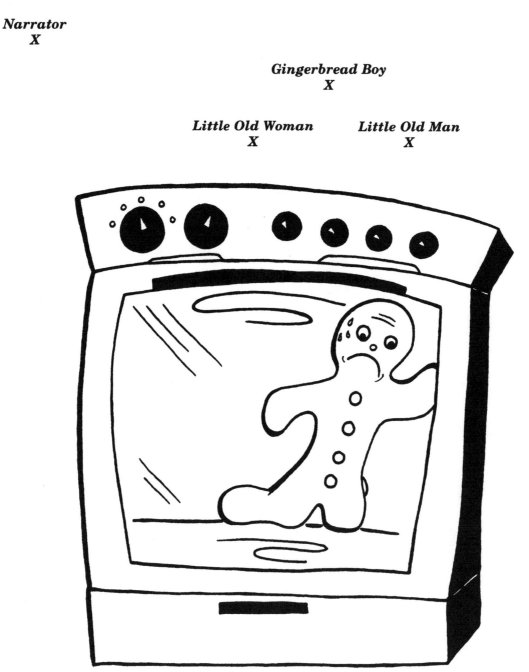

NARRATOR: Once upon a time there was a little old woman and a little old man. They lived all alone in a little old house. One day, the little old woman decided to make a gingerbread boy. I guess she thought the gingerbread boy would become her son. I guess she's a crazy little old woman.

LITTLE OLD WOMAN: Well, now I'm finished mixing the flour, butter, sugar, ginger, and all the other ingredients. I think I'll shape this into a little gingerbread boy.

LITTLE OLD MAN: Why are you doing that, my little crazy old woman?

LITTLE OLD WOMAN: Because we don't have a son of our own, my crazy little old man.

LITTLE OLD MAN: I think the narrator is right. I think you are crazy.

LITTLE OLD WOMAN: Never mind what the narrator said! I'm just going to put this little gingerbread boy into the oven and bake him for about 15 to 20 minutes at 350 degrees. Then maybe we'll eat him up for dinner.

NARRATOR: The little old woman preheated her oven, and put the cookie sheet with the little gingerbread boy on it into the oven. After that, she and the little old man went into the living room to watch a couple of really neat videos on MTV. Unfortunately, the little old lady forgot to set the timer on the oven.

GINGERBREAD BOY: Hey, it's really getting warm in here. I hope that crazy old lady doesn't forget about me.

NARRATOR: Several minutes pass.

GINGERBREAD BOY: It's getting hotter and hotter in here. I'm really beginning to sweat like a pig.

NARRATOR: More time passes.

GINGERBREAD BOY: Wow!!! I'm really getting hot in here. I'm burning up all over my body. *(shouting)* Help!! Let me out. Come on, crazy old woman, let me out of here. I can't stand it anymore.

POSSIBLE CONCLUSIONS

1. The gingerbread boy gets burned to a crisp, and the little old woman feeds the crumbs to the birds.

2. The little old man goes into the kitchen for a glass of milk, notices the gingerbread boy burning up, and rescues him.

3. The gingerbread boy explodes inside the oven, and the little old woman has to spend three weeks cleaning up the mess.

4. The gingerbread boy finds a small crack in the door of the oven and escapes. He runs away and has a strange adventure with a fox.

5. Your idea.

Part V

APPENDIXES

**(The stuff you always find
at the end of a book)**

APPENDIX A: Here's a Bunch of FAIRY TALES, MOTHER GOOSE RHYMES, FOLK TALES, AND OTHER REALLY NEAT STORIES (from "Once upon a Time" Time) to Share with KIDS and OTHER HUMAN BEINGS

Aesop. *Aesop's Fables*. New York: Viking, 1981.

Alderson, Brian, ed. *Cakes and Custard: Children's Rhymes*. New York: Morrow Junior Books, 1975.

Andersen, Hans Christian. *Thumbelina*. New York: Dial Books for Young Readers, 1979.

———. *The Ugly Duckling*. New York: Harcourt Brace Jovanovich, 1979.

Asbjørnsen, Peter Christian, and Jorgen E. Moe. *Three Billy Goats Gruff*. New York: Clarion Books, 1981.

Brett, Jan. *Beauty and the Beast*. New York: Clarion Books, 1989.

———. *Goldilocks and the Three Bears*. New York: Dodd, Mead, 1987.

Briggs, Raymond. *The Mother Goose Treasury*. New York: Coward-McCann, 1966.

Cauley, Lorinda Bryan. *Goldilocks and the Three Bears*. New York: Putnam, 1981.

———. *The Town Mouse and the Country Mouse*. New York: Putnam, 1984.

Cole, Joanna, and Stephanie Calmenson. *Miss Mary Mac: And Other Children's Street Rhymes*. New York: Morrow Junior Books, 1990.

De Beaumont, Madame Le Prince. *Beauty and the Beast*. New York: Crown, 1986.

dePaola, Tomie. *The Comic Adventures of Old Mother Hubbard and Her Dog*. San Diego, Calif.: Harcourt Brace Jovanovich, 1981.

———. *Tomie dePaola's Favorite Nursery Tales*. New York: Putnam, 1986.

———. *Tomie dePaola's Mother Goose*. New York: G. P. Putnam's Sons, 1985.

De Regniers, Beatrice Schenk. *Red Riding Hood: Retold in Verse*. New York: Atheneum, 1977.

Domanska, Janina. *Little Red Hen*. New York: Macmillan, 1973.

Edens, Cooper, ed. *The Glorious Mother Goose*. New York: Atheneum, 1988.

Emberley, Barbara. *The Story of Paul Bunyan*. Englewood Cliffs, N.J.: Prentice-Hall, 1963.

Galdone, Paul. *Cinderella*. New York: McGraw-Hill, 1978.

———. *The Gingerbread Boy*. New York: Clarion Books, 1983.

———. *The Hare and the Tortoise*. New York: McGraw-Hill, 1962.

———. *Henny Penny*. New York: Clarion Books, 1984.

———. *Jack and the Beanstalk*. New York: Clarion Books, 1982.

———. *Little Bo-Peep*. New York: Clarion Books, 1982.

———. *The Little Red Hen*. New York: McGraw-Hill, 1985.

————. *Little Red Riding Hood*. New York: McGraw-Hill, 1974.

————. *The Magic Porridge Pot*. New York: Clarion Books, 1976.

————. *Old Mother Hubbard and Her Dog*. New York: McGraw-Hill, 1960.

————. *Rumplestiltskin*. New York: Clarion Books, 1985.

————. *Three Aesop Fox Fables*. New York: Clarion Books, 1971.

————. *The Three Bears*. New York: Clarion Books, 1985.

————. *Three Little Kittens*. New York: Clarion Books, 1986.

————. *The Three Little Pigs*. New York: Clarion Books, 1984.

Greenaway, Kate. *Mother Goose: Or, the Old Nursery Rhymes*. New York: Warne, 1981.

Griego, Morgot C., Betsy L. Bucks, Sharon S. Gilbert, and Laurel H. Kimball. *Tortillas Para Mama and Other Spanish Nursery Rhymes*. New York: Holt, Rinehart & Winston, 1981.

Grimm, Jakob, and Wilhelm Grimm. *The Bremen Town Musicians*. New York: Harper & Row, 1987.

————. *Cinderella*. New York: Greenwillow Books, 1981.

————. *The Donkey Prince*. New York: Doubleday, 1977.

————. *The Elves and the Shoemaker*. Chicago: Follett, 1967.

————. *Favorite Tales from Grimm*. New York: Four Winds Press, 1982.

————. *The Frog Prince*. New York: Scholastic, 1987.

————. *Grimm's Fairy Tales: Twenty Stories Illustrated by Arthur Rackham*. New York: Viking, 1973.

————. *Hansel and Gretel*. New York: Morrow Junior Books, 1980.

————. *Little Red Riding Hood*. New York: Atheneum, 1988.

————. *Popular Folk Tales: The Brothers Grimm*. New York: Doubleday, 1978.

————. *Rapunzel*. New York: Holiday House, 1987.

————. *Rumplestiltskin*. New York: Four Winds Press, 1973.

————. *The Shoemaker and the Elves*. New York: Lothrop, Lee & Shepard, 1983.

————. *The Sleeping Beauty*. New York: Atheneum, 1979.

————. *Snow White*. Boston: Little, Brown, 1974.

————. *Snow White and Rose Red*. New York: Delacorte Press, 1965.

————. *Snow White and the Seven Dwarfs*. New York: Farrar, Straus & Giroux, 1987.

————. *Tom Thumb*. New York: Walck, 1974.

Hague, Michael, ed. *Mother Goose*. New York: Holt, Rinehart & Winston, 1984.

Hale, Sara. *Mary Had a Little Lamb*. New York: Holiday House, 1984.

Haley, Gail. *Jack and the Bean Tree*. New York: Crown, 1986.

Harper, Wilhelmina. *The Gunniwolf*. New York: E. P. Dutton, 1967.

Hayes, Sarah. *Bad Egg: The True Story of Humpty Dumpty*. Boston: Little, Brown, 1987.

Hutchinson, Veronica S. *Henny Penny*. Boston: Little, Brown, 1976.

Ivimey, John W. *The Complete Story of the Three Blind Mice*. New York: Clarion Books, 1987.

Jacobs, Joseph. *Jack and the Beanstalk*. New York: G. P. Putnam's Sons, 1983.

————. *The Three Little Pigs*. New York: Atheneum, 1980.

Jeffers, Susan. *If Wishes Were Horses: Mother Goose Rhymes*. New York: E. P. Dutton, 1979.

Kellogg, Steven. *Chicken Little*. New York: Morrow Junior Books, 1985.

————. *Paul Bunyan*. New York: Morrow Junior Books, 1974.

————. *Pecos Bill*. New York: Morrow Junior Books, 1986.

Lobel, Arnold. *Gregory Griggs and Other Nursery Rhyme People*. New York: Greenwillow Books, 1978.

————. *The Random House Book of Mother Goose*. New York: Random House, 1986.

Marshall, James. *Goldilocks and the Three Bears*. New York: Dial Books for Young Readers, 1988.

————. *James Marshall's Mother Goose*. New York: Farray, Straus & Giroux, 1979.

————. *Red Riding Hood*. New York: Dial, 1987.

Martin, Sarah. *The Comic Adventures of Old Mother Hubbard and Her Dog*. San Diego, Calif.: Harcourt Brace Jovanovich, 1981.

Miller, Mitchell. *One Misty Moisty Morning*. New York: Farrar, Straus & Giroux, 1971.

Newbery, John. *The Original Mother Goose's Melody*. New York: Gale Research, 1969.

Opie, Iona, and Peter Opie. *A Nursery Companion*. London: Oxford University Press, 1980.

————. *The Oxford Nursery Rhyme Book*. London: Oxford University Press, 1984.

———. *Tail Feathers from Mother Goose: The Opie Rhyme Book*. Boston: Little, Brown, 1988.

Ormerod, Jan. *The Story of Chicken Licken*. New York: Lothrop, Lee & Shepard, 1986.

Oxenbury, Helen. *The Helen Oxenbury Nursery Story Book*. New York: Alfred A. Knopf, 1985.

Pearson, Tracey. *Old Macdonald Had a Farm*. New York: Dial Books for Young Readers, 1984.

Perrault, Charles. *Cinderella*. New York: Dial Books for Young Readers, 1985.

———. *Little Red Riding Hood*. New York: Scholastic, 1971.

———. *Puss in Boots*. New York: Clarion Books, 1976.

———. *The Sleeping Beauty*. New York: Viking, 1972.

Provensen, Alice, and Martin Provensen. *Old Mother Hubbard*. New York: Random House, 1982.

Rounds, Glen. *Old Macdonald Had a Farm*. New York: Holiday House, 1989.

Southey, Robert. *The Three Bears*. New York: G. P. Putnam's Sons, 1984.

Spier, Peter. *London Bridge Is Falling Down*. New York: Doubleday, 1967.

Stevens, Janet. *Goldilocks and the Three Bears*. New York: Holiday House, 1986.

———. *The House That Jack Built*. New York: Holiday House, 1985.

Still, James. *Jack and the Wonder Beans*. New York: G. P. Putnam's Sons, 1977.

Tarrant, Margaret. *Nursery Rhymes*. New York: Thomas Y. Crowell, 1978.

Thompson, Pat, ed. *Rhymes Around the Day*. New York: Lothrop, Lee & Shepard, 1983.

Tripp, Wallace. *Granfa' Grig Had a Pig and Other Rhymes Without Reason from Mother Goose*. Boston: Little, Brown, 1976.

Tudor, Tasha. *Mother Goose*. New York: Walck, 1972.

Watson, Wendy. *Wendy Watson's Mother Goose*. New York: Lothrop, Lee & Shepard, 1989.

Watts, Bernadette. *Goldilocks and the Three Bears*. New York: Holt, Rinehart & Winston, 1985.

Wildsmith, Brian. *Brian Wildsmith's Mother Goose*. New York: Oxford University Press, 1982.

Zuromskis, Diane. *The Farmer in the Dell*. Boston: Little, Brown, 1978.

APPENDIX B: Wow! This Is Unbelievable! Here's a LIST of Several FAR-OUT and FUNKY TITLES Students Can Use to Create Their Own READERS THEATRE SCRIPTS (From Scratch, of Course)

Are you still with me? If so, I've got some other titles your students might like to experiment with in developing and designing their own readers theatre scripts.

I have often found it advantageous to divide my class into small groups and encourage each team to first brainstorm for as many stories, legends, and Mother Goose rhymes as they can remember. All of these are recorded on the chalkboard. Then, groups are encouraged to develop weird and wacky tales for selected stories. These are also shared with the whole class. Later, each group will select its favorite title and begin creating a readers theatre script. This approach supports a process approach to writing and stimulates an atmosphere of creative thinking.

Although you are certainly encouraged to use some of these suggested titles, it will be valuable for your students to have opportunities to generate their own titles. No doubt they will come up with some equally weird and strange titles for their stories (as well as some equally weird and strange stories). What you will discover is students who are not only immersed in the creativity of readers theatre but who want to use all of their language arts skills (reading, writing, speaking, listening) in meaningful and productive contexts.

1. Pat-a-Cake, Pat-a-Cake Baker's Man! Make Me a Cheeseburger with Fries and a Coke as Fast as You Can

2. Here We Go 'Round the Mulberry Bush (and What the Heck Is a Mulberry Bush?)

3. Roses Are Red, Violets Are Blue, This Story Is Crazy, and So Are You

4. Rub-a-Dub-Dub, Three Men in a Tub (and How Did They Get There in the First Place?)

5. The Farmer in the Dell, the Farmer in the Dell, Hi Ho the Derry-O, the Farmer in (Hey, This Doesn't Make Any Sense)

6. Humpty Dumpty Gets Scrambled at McDonald's

7. The Ugly Duckling Turns into the Pretty Good-Looking Duckling

8. The Three Little Pigs Blow Down the Wolf's House

9. Chicken Little Is Found at the Local KFC Restaurant

10. One, Two, Buckle My Shoe; Three, Four, I Hit My Head on the Floor

11. Jack Be Nimble, Jack Be Quick, Jack Jumped over the Candlestick and Burned off All the Hair on His Legs

12. Little Red Riding Hood Makes a Big Mistake and Eats Her Grandmother

13. Mary Had a Little Lamb That Grew up to Become a Big, Bad Sheep

14. Mary, Mary, Quite Contrary, How Does Your Garden Grow? With Lots of Weeds and Too Few Seeds

15. Tom, Tom, the Piper's Son, Stole a Pig, but Just Couldn't Lift It

16. Tweedle-Dum and Tweedle-Dee Sit in Class in Front of Me

17. Moses Supposes His Toeses Are Roses (Perhaps Somebody Better Talk to Moses)

18. Rain, Rain, Go Away, Today Is Saturday—I Want to Play!

19. Georgie Porgie, Pudding and Pie, Kissed the Girls and Got into Lots of Trouble with the Principal

20. This Little Piggy Went to Market and Was Amazed at the Price of Everything

21. A Big, Giant Spider, Sat on a Tuffet, and Scared Miss Muffet and the Whole Second-Grade Class

22. Silly Sally Sipped a Slew of Salted Sodas, a Slew of Salted Sodas Silly Sally Sipped

23. The Owl and the Pussycat Went to Sea, but They Didn't Catch a Single Fish

24. One for the Money, Two for the Show, Boy This Counting Sure Is Slow

25. Hot Cross Buns, Hot Cross Buns, What the Heck Are Hot Cross Buns?

25. Three Little Kittens Lost Their Mittens and Had to Stay After School Until They Found Them

26. Pease Porridge Hot, Pease Porridge Cold, Pease Porridge in the Pot, Nine Days Old (Oh, Yuck!!!)

27. Sing a Song of Sixpence, a Pocket Full of Rye (and How Did All That Rye Get in My Pocket?)

28. Humpty Dumpty Sat on a Wall—and How Did He Get on the Wall in the First Place?

29. Little Boy Blue, Come Blow Your Horn! Recess Is Over, It's Time for Spelling

30. Wee Willie Winkie Runs Through the Town, but Nobody Knows Why He Does That

31. The Three Pigs Move to a New Neighborhood

32. Hansel and Gretel Move to a New Forest

33.   Snow White Tells Everybody Her Real Name

34.   The Three Bears Become New Students in Mrs. Smith's Third-Grade Class

35.   Chicken Little Gets Fried for Dinner

36.   Beauty and the Beast Get Married and Move to Los Angeles

37.   Mother Goose Is Really a Duck in Disguise

APPENDIX C: Some ARTICLES and BOOKS and Other Things About READERS THEATRE You Might Want to Look At in Your Copious Free Time

Magazine Articles About Readers Theatre

Busching, B. A. "Readers Theatre: An Education for Language and Life." *Language Arts* 58 (1981): 330-38.

Henning, K. "Drama Reading: An Ongoing Classroom Activity at the Elementary School Level." *Elementary English* 51 (1974): 48-51.

Post, R. M. "Readers Theatre as a Method of Teaching Literature." *English Journal* 64 (1974): 69-72.

Wertheimer, A. "Story Dramatization in the Reading Center." *English Journal* 64 (1974): 85-87.

Books About Readers Theatre

Coger, L. I., and M. R. White. *Readers Theatre Handbook: A Dramatic Approach to Literature.* Glenview, Ill.: Scott, Foresman, 1982.

Dixon, N., A. Davies, and C. Politano. *Learning with Readers Theatre: Building Connections.* Winnipeg, Ont., Canada: Peguis, 1996.

Johnson, T. D., and D. R. Louis. *Bring It All Together: A Program for Literacy.* Portsmouth, N.H.: Heinemann, 1990.

Maclay, J. H. *Readers Theatre: Toward a Grammar of Practice.* New York: Random House, 1971.

Shepard, A. *Stories on Stage: Scripts for Reader's Theatre.* New York: H. W. Wilson, 1993.

Sloyer, S. *Readers Theatre: Story Dramatization in the Classroom.* Urbana, Ill.: National Council for Teachers of English, 1982.

Tanner, F. *Creative Communication: Projects in Acting, Speaking, Oral Reading.* Pocatello, Idaho: Clark, 1979.

Sources for Additional Readers Theatre Scripts

Barchers, S. *Fifty Fabulous Fables: Beginning Readers Theatre.* Englewood, Colo.: Teacher Ideas Press, 1997.

———. *Readers Theatre for Beginning Readers.* Englewood, Colo.: Teacher Ideas Press, 1993.

———. *Scary Readers Theatre.* Englewood, Colo.: Teacher Ideas Press, 1994.

Criscoe, B. L., and P. J. Lanasa. *Fairy Tales for Two Readers.* Englewood, Colo.: Teacher Ideas Press, 1995.

Fredericks, A. D. *Frantic Frogs and Other Frankly Fractured Folktales for Readers Theatre.* Englewood, Colo.: Teacher Ideas Press, 1993.

Georges, C., and C. Cornett. *Reader's Theatre.* Buffalo, N.Y.: D. O. K., 1990.

Haven, K. *Great Moments in Science: Experiments and Readers Theatre.* Englewood, Colo.: Teacher Ideas Press, 1996.

Latrobe, K. H., C. Casey, and L. A. Gann. *Social Studies Readers Theatre for Young Adults.* Englewood, Colo.: Teacher Ideas Press, 1991.

Latrobe, K. H., and M. K. Laughlin. *Readers Theatre for Young Adults.* Englewood, Colo.: Teacher Ideas Press, 1989.

Laughlin, M. K., P. T. Black, and K. H. Latrobe. *Social Studies Readers Theatre for Children.* Englewood, Colo.: Teacher Ideas Press, 1991.

Laughlin, M. K., and K. H. Latrobe. *Readers Theatre for Children.* Englewood, Colo.: Teacher Ideas Press, 1990.

Pfeffinger, C. R. *Holiday Readers Theatre.* Englewood, Colo.: Teacher Ideas Press, 1994.

Reader's Theatre Script Service, P.O. Box 178333, San Diego, CA 92177; (619) 276-1948.

Web Sites

http://www.aaronshep.com/rt/rte.html
    Offers ways to use readers theatre, sample scripts from a children's author who specializes in readers theatre, and an extensive list of resources.

http://mcrel.org/connect/plus/theatre.html
    Provides lesson plan activities, teacher's guides, ways to adapt stories to a readers theatre format, and on-line children's stories.

http://www.booklures.com/readthe.html
    Presents information on readers theatre and accompanying activities, readers theatre book talks, and multicultural readers theatre.

http://www.vquest.com/rtheatre
    Describes an organization dedicated to the development and use of readers theatre in education.

Professional Organizations

Readers Theatre International
    P.O. Box 65059
    North Hill, R.P.O.
    Calgary, Canada AB T2N 4T6
    (403) 220-1770
    Toll free: (888) 221-1770

Institute for Readers Theatre
    P.O. Box 178333
    San Diego, CA 92177
    (619) 276-1948

About the Author
(This Is the Really Scary Part)

Anthony D. Fredericks

OK, OK, let's get one thing straight—this guy is no enchanted prince. After all, he wears glasses (he hasn't quite figured out how to stick contacts onto his eyeballs), he's balding on top (the result of a dip in the wrong gene pool), and he wears a tie (when was the last time you ever saw a prince in a tie?). True, he does have that perpetual smile plastered on his face, but so do a lot of insurance salespeople and used car dealers.

Here's what we do know about Tony: His background includes more than 25 years of experience as a classroom teacher, reading specialist, curriculum coordinator, staff developer, author, professional story-teller, and college professor ("Oh, no, not one of those!"). In addition, Tony visits hundreds of classrooms and schools throughout the country working with teachers and students on effective teaching/learning strategies. He has written more than 30 teacher resource books on language arts, science, and social studies topics. Additionally, he's authored a half-dozen highly acclaimed children's books about animals and environmental studies (e.g., *Clever Camouflagers* and *Exploring the Rainforest*).

Tony currently teaches elementary methods courses at York College in York, Pennsylvania (where students have never referred to him as a prince, enchanted or otherwise). His best friends include a little girl who keeps bringing farm animals to school, a cow with aspirations of becoming an Olympic high jumper, and a guy who spends his entire life living in used vegetables. His wife—truly a beautiful enchanted princess—continues to question his state of mind.